NEED to KNOW

EDEXCEL A-LEVEL ECONOMICS

Key facts at your fingertips

David Horner

Steve Stoddard

HODDER
EDUCATION
AN HACHETTE UK COMPANY

Hachette UK's policy is to use papers that are natural, renewable and recyclable products and made from wood grown in sustainable forests. The logging and manufacturing processes are expected to conform to the environmental regulations of the country of origin.

Orders: please contact Bookpoint Ltd, 130 Park Drive, Milton Park, Abingdon, Oxon OX14 4SE. Telephone: (44) 01235 827827. Fax: (44) 01235 400401. Email: education@bookpoint.co.uk

Lines are open from 9 a.m. to 5 p.m., Monday to Saturday, with a 24-hour message answering service. You can also order through our website: www. hoddereducation.co.uk

ISBN: 978 1 5104 2852 2

First published in 2018 by
Hodder Education,
An Hachette UK Company
Carmelite House
50 Victoria Embankment
London EC4Y 0DZ

Impression number   10 9 8 7 6 5 4 3 2 1

Year   2022 2021 2020 2019 2018

Typeset by Aptara

Printed in Spain

A catalogue record for this title is available from the British Library.

MIX
Paper from
responsible sources
FSC™ C104740
FSC
www.fsc.org

Contents

Getting the most from this book

This *Need to Know* guide is designed to help you throughout your course as a companion to your learning and a revision aid in the months or weeks leading up to the final exams.

The following features in each section will help you get the most from the book.

You need to know

Each topic begins with a list summarising what you 'need to know' in this topic for the exam.

Exam tip

Key knowledge you need to demonstrate in the exam, tips on exam technique, common misconceptions to avoid and important things to remember.

Key terms

Definitions of highlighted terms in the text to make sure you know the essential terminology for your subject.

Do you know?

Questions at the end of each topic to test you on some of its key points. Check your answers here: www.hoddereducation.co.uk/needtoknow/answers

Synoptic links

Reminders of how knowledge and skills from different topics in your A-level relate to one another.

End of section questions

Questions at the end of each main section of the book to test your knowledge of the specification area covered. Check your answers here: www.hoddereducation.co.uk/needtoknow/answers

1 Introduction to markets and market failure

1.1 The nature of economics

You need to know

- economics as a social science
- positive and normative economic statements
- the economic problem
- production possibility frontiers (PPFs)
- specialisation and the division of labour
- free market economies, mixed economies and command economies

Economics as a social science

Economics:

- studies how the world's scarce resources are allocated to competing uses to satisfy society's wants
- attempts to use scientific methodology for observing human behaviour and then makes predictions
- builds predictive models on the basis that all other variables are held constant, known as the **ceteris paribus** assumption

Key terms

Ceteris paribus Assuming all other variables are held constant.

Positive statement An objective statement that can be tested against the facts to be declared either true or false.

Normative statement A subjective opinion or value judgement that cannot be declared either true or false.

Exam tip

A positive statement need not necessarily be factually true. It simply needs to be capable of being tested to be declared true or false.

Synoptic link

Improving the quality and quantity of the four factors of production is the key to economic growth at a macroeconomic level.

The economic problem

The problem of scarcity

- Scarcity means economic resources are limited relative to society's wants.
- Choices are made when allocating resources.

- We must consider the three fundamental economic questions:
  - □ *What* to produce and in what quantities?
  - □ *How* should goods and services be produced?
  - □ *To whom* should goods and services be allocated?

Economic resources

- A country's resources are referred to as **factors of production**.
- Renewable resources can be replaced naturally after use, e.g. solar energy.
- Non-renewable resources are those that will eventually be exhausted, e.g. oil.

Key term

Factors of production
A country's productive economic resources, divided into capital, enterprise, land and labour.

Factor of production	Definition	Example
Capital	Manmade physical equipment used to make other goods and services	Machinery and computer equipment
Enterprise	Individuals who take a business risk in combining the other three factors of production in order to produce a good or service	Jeff Bezos, Richard Branson, James Dyson, Karren Brady, Deborah Meaden, Michelle Mone
Land	All naturally occurring resources	Minerals, the sea, fertile land and the environment
Labour	People involved in production, sometimes referred to as human capital	Teacher, accountant, farmer

Opportunity cost, economic goods and free goods

Key terms

Opportunity cost The cost of the next best alternative you give up when you have to make a choice.

Economic good A good that has an opportunity cost in consumption because it uses up scarce resources, e.g. most consumer goods.

Free good A good that does not have an opportunity cost in consumption because it does not use up scarce resources, e.g. sunlight or air.

Exam tip

The four factors of production can be memorised using the acronym CELL, standing for capital, enterprise, land and labour.

Production possibility frontiers

Figure 1 shows a **production possibility frontier (PPF)**.

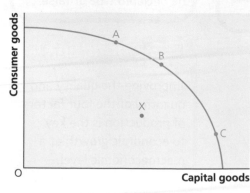

Figure 1 A production possibility frontier

Key term

Production possibility frontier (PPF) A diagram that shows the maximum possible output combinations of two goods in an economy, assuming full employment of efficient resources.

- In constructing this PPF it is assumed the economy can produce either **capital goods** or **consumer goods**.
- Any point on the production possibility curve, e.g. A, B or C, means all factors of production are fully employed.
- An economy operating at point X is operating inefficiently, with unused resources, e.g. unemployed labour.
- Any points to the right of the PPF are currently unobtainable, but could be reached with **economic growth**.

Using a PPF diagram to show opportunity cost

The PPF in Figure 2 shows the concept of opportunity cost.

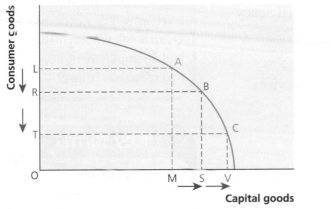

Figure 2 Production possibility frontiers and opportunity costs

Shifts of the PPF

Factors causing an outward shift of the PPF	Factors causing an inward shift of the PPF
Technological improvements	Natural disasters, e.g. earthquakes or floods
Discovery of new resources, e.g. oil and gas	Wars
Improvements in education and training	Global warming/climate change leading to loss of farmland, rising sea levels and extreme weather
Demographic changes, e.g. increases in immigration or an increased retirement age	A prolonged recession, which may lead to permanent loss of productive capacity

Using a PPF diagram to show economic growth

An improvement in technology or any of the factors that lead to an outward shift of the PPF, as shown in Figure 3, means that there has been an increase in the productive capacity of the economy (i.e. economic growth).

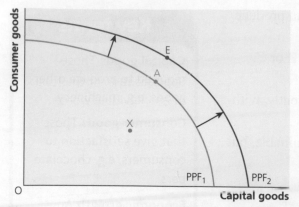

Figure 3 Production possibility frontiers and economic growth

Economic efficiency and PPF diagrams

The concepts of **productive efficiency** and productive inefficiency are shown in Figure 4.

The **allocatively efficient** point on the PPF is the one that best reflects society's preferences for particular goods and services.

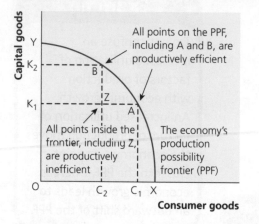

All points on the PPF, including A and B, are productively efficient

All points inside the frontier, including Z, are productively inefficient

The economy's production possibility frontier (PPF)

Figure 4 Productive efficiency and the PPF

Specialisation and the division of labour

Specialisation is:

■ where an individual worker, firm, region or country produces a limited range of goods or services, e.g.:

  □ an individual worker specialising as a tax accountant
  □ an individual firm specialising in accountancy, e.g. PwC
  □ an individual region specialising in investment banking, e.g. the City of London
  □ an individual country specialising in the provision of financial services, e.g. the UK

Division of labour is specialisation at the level of the individual worker, as identified by Adam Smith in *The Wealth of Nations*

Advantages and disadvantages of specialisation and division of labour

Advantages	Disadvantages
Reduced time spent moving between different tasks or workstations means increased productivity	Monotony and boredom, leading to reduced productivity
Repetition of a limited range of activities can increase skill and aptitude, leading to a worker becoming an expert, e.g. a leading neurosurgeon	Loss of skills
As tasks are broken up into smaller ones, it becomes efficient to use specialist machinery	Strikes could stop production
Allows people to work to their natural strengths	

The functions of money

- A medium of exchange
- A store of value
- A measure of value
- A means of deferred payment

Free market economies, mixed economies and command economies

- Free market or capitalist economy: decisions made solely by the interactions of consumers and firms, with no government intervention.
- Mixed economy: some decisions regarding resource allocation are made by the free market while others are made by government.
- Command or centrally planned economy: decisions made solely by governments.

Market economies		Command economies	
Advantages	Disadvantages	Advantages	Disadvantages
Consumer sovereignty	Inequality	Equality	Inefficiency
Flexibility	Imperfect information	Macroeconomic stability	Lack of incentives
Competition	Externalities	Fewer externalities	Reduced choice
Choice	Monopolies	Full employment	Shortages and surpluses
Economic and political freedom	Macroeconomic instability		

Do you know?

1 Explain why economics is referred to as a social science.
2 Explain the difference between positive and normative economic statements.
3 State and give examples of each of the four factors of production.
4 State and explain the economic problem.
5 Sketch a PPF diagram and use it to show the following: productive efficiency, opportunity cost, economic growth.
6 Compare the advantages and disadvantages of a free market economy and a command economy.

1.2 How markets work

You need to know

- rational decision-making
- demand, including price elasticity of demand, income elasticity of demand and cross elasticity of demand
- supply, including price elasticity of supply
- price determination and the price mechanism
- consumer and producer surplus
- indirect taxes and subsidies
- alternative views of consumer behaviour

Rational decision-making

- Traditional, neoclassical economic theory assumes consumers always act rationally, seeking to maximise satisfaction for every pound spent.

- **Utility** is the amount of satisfaction or benefit that a consumer gains from consuming a good or service.
- **Rational consumers** will consume a good or service if the perceived satisfaction is greater than or equal to price.

Demand

Economists are concerned with **effective demand**.

Shape of the demand curve

- The 'law' of **demand** states that as the price of a good or service falls, the quantity demanded increases.
- This inverse relationship between the price and quantity demanded of a good or service is shown in Figure 5.
- An increase in the quantity demanded resulting from a fall in price is known as an extension of demand, whereas a fall in quantity demanded resulting from an increase in price is known as a contraction in demand.

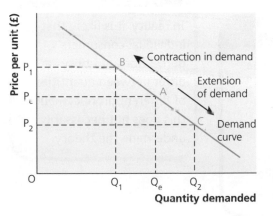

Figure 5 Movements along a demand curve

Shifts in the demand curve

Factors that shift a demand curve:
- real disposable incomes
- tastes and preferences (fashions)
- advertising
- population
- prices of **substitute products**
- prices of **complementary products**
- interest rates

- If any of these conditions of demand change, the demand curve for the good or service will change.
- This leads to a rightward or leftward shift of the demand curve, as shown in Figure 6.
- A rightward shift is an increase in demand, whereas a leftward shift is a decrease in demand.

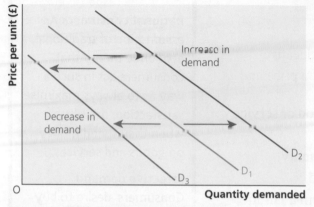

Figure 6 Shifts in the demand curve

> ### Key term
>
> **Conditions of demand** Factors other than the price of the good that lead to a change in position of the demand curve.

Diminishing marginal utility

> ### Key terms
>
> **Total utility** The amount of satisfaction a person derives from the total amount of a product consumed.
>
> **Marginal utility** The satisfaction gained from consuming an additional unit of a good or service.
>
> **Diminishing marginal utility** As individuals consume more units of a good or service, the additional units give successively smaller increases in total satisfaction.

> ### Exam tip
>
> In reality, it is likely that individual consumers' perceptions of utility differ between quantities of different products, but this does not necessarily undermine the theory.

- Diminishing marginal utility is a way of deriving an individual's downward-sloping demand curve for a good or service, as shown in Figure 7.
- As marginal utility declines, the price the consumer is willing to pay for additional units decreases.

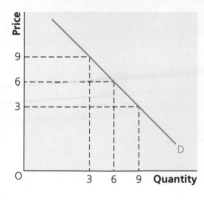

Figure 7 Diminishing marginal utility and the individual demand curve

> ### Exam tip
>
> It is worth memorising the percentage change formula as you will be required to use it frequently.
>
> $$\text{percentage change} = \frac{\text{change}}{\text{original value}} \times 100$$

Price elasticity of demand

Measurement of price elasticity of demand

Key term

Price elasticity of demand (PED) The responsiveness of quantity demanded of a good to a change in price.

- The formula for **price elasticity of demand (PED)** is:

$$PED = \frac{\text{percentage change in quantity demanded}}{\text{percentage change in price}}$$

- The value for price elasticity of demand is usually negative because of the assumed inverse relationship between price and quantity demanded.
- We tend to ignore the minus sign in any calculation.

Key values, explanations and diagrams

Term	Explanation	Example
Price inelastic demand	When demand is price inelastic, the value of PED is between 0 and 1, ignoring the minus sign. Figure 8(a) illustrates an inelastic section of a demand curve	A 50% increase in the price of petrol leads to a 10% fall in quantity demanded $PED = \frac{-10}{+50} = -0.2$
Price elastic demand	When demand is price elastic, the value of PED is greater than 1, ignoring the minus sign. Figure 8(b) illustrates an elastic section of a demand curve	A 10% reduction in the price of cars leads to a 15% increase in quantity demanded $PED = \frac{+15}{-10} = -1.5$
Unitary elastic demand	When demand is unitary elastic, the value of PED is exactly 1, ignoring the minus sign. The demand curve is a rectangular hyperbola, as shown in Figure 9	A 20% increase in the price of a mobile phone leads to a 20% decrease in quantity demanded $PED = \frac{-20}{+20} = -1.0$
Perfectly inelastic demand	When demand is perfectly inelastic, the value of PED is 0. The demand curve will be vertical, as shown in Figure 9	A 10% increase in the price of a carton of milk leads to no change in quantity demanded $PED = \frac{0}{+10} = 0.0$
Perfectly elastic demand	When demand is perfectly elastic, the value of PED is infinity. The demand curve will be horizontal, as shown in Figure 9	An extremely small increase in the price of a product leads to the quantity demanded falling to zero

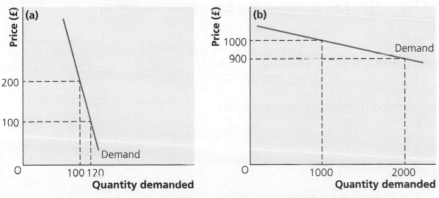

Figure 8 (a) An inelastic and (b) an elastic section of a demand curve

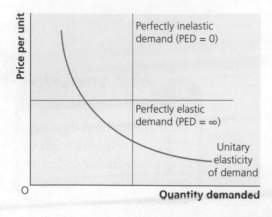

Figure 9 Demand curves showing unitary elasticity, perfectly inelastic and perfectly elastic demand

Factors influencing PED

- Availability of close substitutes
- Percentage of income spent on the product
- Nature of the product
- Durability of the product
- Time period
- Broad or specific market definition

PED and total revenue

- The PED of a product determines what happens to consumer spending (and therefore total revenue) following a price change.
  - ☐ If demand is price elastic, a reduction in price leads to an increase in total revenue.
  - ☐ If demand is price inelastic, a reduction in price leads to a decrease in total revenue.
  - ☐ If demand is price elastic, a price increase leads to a reduction in total revenue.
  - ☐ If demand is price inelastic, a price increase leads to an increase in total revenue.

Significance of PED for firms and governments

- If demand is price inelastic, firms can increase revenue by increasing price.
- Governments can maximise tax revenue by placing indirect taxes on inelastic goods.

Income elasticity of demand

- The formula for income elasticity of demand (YED) is:

$$YED = \frac{\text{percentage change in quantity demanded}}{\text{percentage change in real income}}$$

Key values and explanations

- For YED the sign is important.
- If the value is positive, i.e. greater than 0, the product is a normal good. This means a rise in income will lead to an increase in demand.
- If the value is negative, i.e. less than 0, the product is an inferior good. This means a rise in income will lead to a fall in demand.

Term	Explanation	Example
Income elastic demand	When demand is income elastic, the value of YED is greater than +1. Income elastic products are often referred to as luxury goods	A 10% increase in real income leads to a 20% increase in demand for foreign holidays $$YED = \frac{+20}{+10} = +2.0$$
Income inelastic demand	When demand is income inelastic, the value of YED is between 0 and +1. Income inelastic products are often referred to as basic goods or necessities	A 10% increase in real income leads to a 2% increase in demand for cartons of milk $$YED = \frac{+2}{+10} = +0.2$$
Negative income elastic demand	When demand is negative income elastic, the value of YED is negative, i.e. less than 0. Negative income elastic products are referred to as inferior goods	A 20% increase in real income leads to a 10% fall in demand for a supermarket's value brand of baked beans $$YED = \frac{-10}{+20} = -0.5$$

Significance of YED for firms and governments

- If firms know that their products are income elastic, they can expect revenues to increase during periods of economic growth but fall during a recession.
- Similarly, governments can maximise tax revenue by placing indirect taxes on income elastic goods during an economic boom.

Cross elasticity of demand

- The formula for **cross elasticity of demand (XED)** is:

$$\text{XED} = \frac{\text{percentage change in quantity demanded of product A}}{\text{percentage change in price of product B}}$$

Key values

- For XED the sign is important.
- A positive value means that products A and B are substitutes, i.e. a rise in the price of product B leads to an increase in demand for product A.
- A negative value means that products A and B are complements, i.e. a rise in price of product B leads to a fall in the demand for product A.
- Example: a 20% increase in the price of cod leads to a 10% fall in the demand for chips.

$$\text{XED} = \frac{-10}{+20} = -0.5$$

The two products are therefore complements.

Significance of XED for firms

- Businesses can use understanding of XED in setting prices, e.g. a close substitute should cut price to increase demand.

Supply

The law of supply

- The law of **supply** states that as price increases, the quantity supplied will increase.
- This positive relationship is shown in Figure 10.

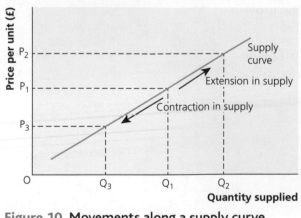

Figure 10 **Movements along a supply curve**

Key terms

Cross elasticity of demand (XED) The responsiveness of the demand for a product following a change in price of another product.

Supply The quantity of a good or service that firms plan to sell at a given price in a particular time period.

- Firms are assumed to want to maximise their profits; a higher price is an incentive to increase production.
- A change in price will lead to a movement along an existing supply curve.
- An increase in price leads to an increase in quantity supplied — an extension of supply.
- A decrease in price leads to a decrease in quantity supplied — a contraction in supply.

Shifts in the supply curve

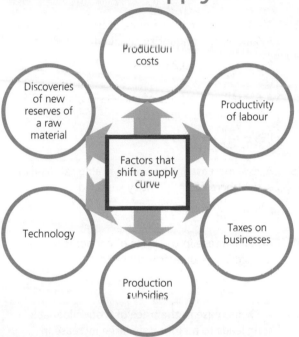

- If any of these conditions of supply change, the supply curve for the good or service will change.
- This leads either to a rightward or leftward shift of the supply curve, as shown in Figure 11.
- A rightward shift is an increase in supply.
- A leftward shift is a decrease in supply.

Key term

Conditions of supply
Factors other than the price of the good that lead to a change in position of the supply curve.

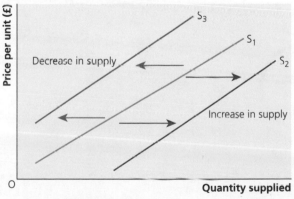

Figure 11 Shifts in the supply curve

Price elasticity of supply

Key term

Price elasticity of supply (PES) The responsiveness of the quantity supplied of a good or service to a change in price.

■ The formula for **price elasticity of supply (PES)** is:

$$PES = \frac{\text{percentage change in quantity supplied}}{\text{percentage change in price}}$$

Key values and explanations

Price elasticity of supply always has a positive value because of the direct relationship between price and quantity supplied.

Term	Explanation	Example
Price inelastic supply	When supply is price inelastic, the value of PES is between 0 and 1 The supply curve will be relatively steep	A 20% increase in the price of barley leads to a 5% increase in quantity supplied $PES = \frac{+5}{+20} = +0.25$
Price elastic supply	When supply is price elastic, the value of PES is greater than 1. The supply curve will be relatively shallow	A 5% fall in the price of carpets leads to a 10% fall in quantity supplied $PES = \frac{-10}{-5} = +2.0$
Unitary elastic supply	When supply is unitary elastic, the value of PES is exactly 1. The supply curve is a straight line drawn through the origin	A 15% increase in the price of table salt leads to a 15% increase in quantity supplied $PES = \frac{+15}{+15} = +1.0$
Perfectly inelastic supply	When supply is perfectly inelastic, the value of PES is 0. The supply curve is vertical	A 5% increase in the price of copper leads to no change in the quantity supplied $PES = \frac{0}{+5} = 0$
Perfectly elastic supply	When supply is perfectly elastic, the value of PES is infinity. The supply curve is horizontal	A 2% increase in the price of a downloadable song leads to an infinitely large increase in quantity supplied

Factors influencing price elasticity of supply

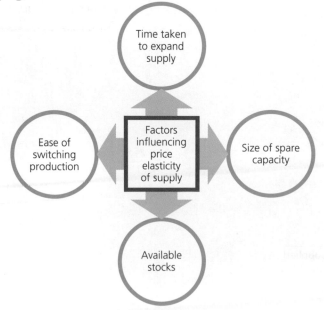

Price determination

Key terms

Market equilibrium price The price at which the planned demand of consumers equals the planned supply of firms.

Market A situation in which buyers and sellers come together to engage in trade.

Market equilibrium A situation where the quantity demanded equals the quantity supplied.

Market disequilibrium A situation where the quantity demanded does not equal the quantity supplied.

Excess supply When the quantity supplied exceeds the quantity demanded, when the price is more than the equilibrium price.

Excess demand When the quantity demanded exceeds the quantity supplied, when the price is less than the equilibrium price.

■ **Market equilibrium price** and quantity are determined by the interaction of the **market** demand and supply curves for a particular good or service, as shown in Figure 12.

■ When quantity demanded equals quantity supplied in a market for a particular product, there is **market equilibrium**.

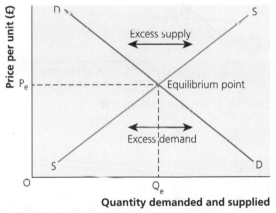

Figure 12 Market equilibrium price and quantity

Excess supply and excess demand

■ **Market disequilibrium** occurs when quantity demanded does not equal quantity supplied, as illustrated in Figure 12.

■ If price is above market equilibrium price (P_e), there is **excess supply**.

■ If price is below market equilibrium price (P_e), there is **excess demand**.

■ Eventually, market forces lead to excess supply or excess demand being resolved.

Changes in the market equilibrium price

■ May be caused by either a shift of the demand curve or a shift of the supply curve (resulting from a change in the conditions of demand or supply).

Term	Explanation	Example
Increase in demand	This will lead to an increase in equilibrium price and quantity, as shown in Figure 13	Following an increase in real incomes, the demand curve of a normal good would shift rightwards
Decrease in demand	This will lead to a decrease in equilibrium price and quantity, as shown in Figure 14	Following a fall in real incomes, the demand curve of a normal good would shift leftwards
Increase in supply	This will lead to a decrease in equilibrium price and an increase in quantity, as shown in Figure 15	Following a good harvest, the supply curve of coffee would shift rightwards
Decrease in supply	This will lead to an increase in equilibrium price and a decrease quantity, as shown in Figure 16	Following a poor harvest, the supply curve of wheat would shift leftwards

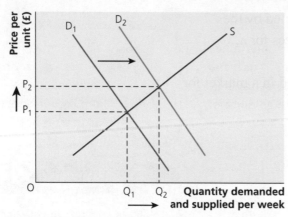

Figure 13 Increase in demand

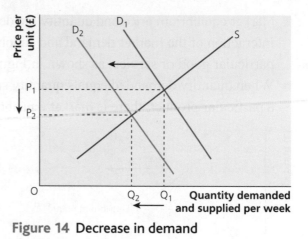

Figure 14 Decrease in demand

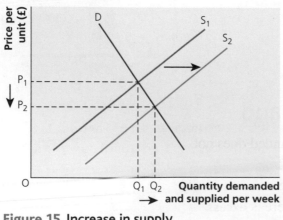

Figure 15 Increase in supply

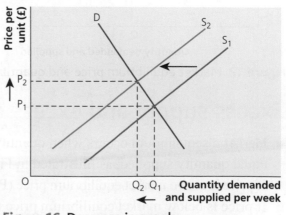

Figure 16 Decrease in supply

The price mechanism

The four functions of prices

- When any of the following key functions of prices breaks down, market failure is said to occur.

Consumer and producer surplus

- Consumer surplus and producer surplus are both concepts of economic welfare.
- Consumer surplus is the surplus value or satisfaction consumers enjoy. In Figure 17 this is equal to the area given by the triangle PAB.

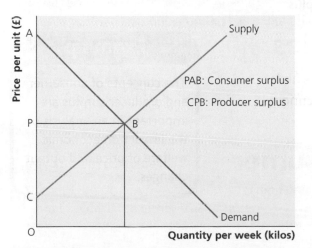

Figure 17 Consumer and producer surplus

- Producer surplus may be regarded as surplus value enjoyed by producers. This is equal to the area given by the triangle CPB in Figure 17.
- Figure 18 shows the effects of an increase in demand on consumer surplus.

■ Figure 19 shows the effects of an increase in supply on producer surplus.

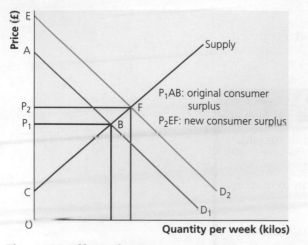

Figure 18 **Effect of an increase in demand on consumer surplus**

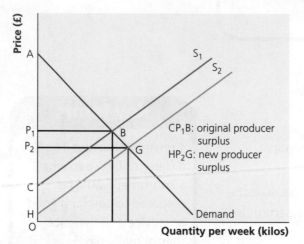

Figure 19 **Effect of an increase in supply on producer surplus**

Indirect taxes and subsidies

See Section 1.4 for explanations, diagrams, advantages and disadvantages of these methods of government intervention.

Alternative views of consumer behaviour

Why consumers may not behave rationally

- The influence of others
- Habitual behaviour
- Inertia
- The inability to process complex information

> **Exam tip**
>
> The concepts of consumer and producer surplus are important in an analysis of the impact on economic welfare of price and output changes.

1.3 Market failure

You need to know

- types of market failure
- externalities
- under-provision of public goods
- information gaps

- **Market failure** is when a market fails to achieve productive efficiency, allocative efficiency or equity.
- It usually arises because the price mechanism has not accounted for all the costs and/or benefits from the production or consumption of a good or service.
- It can be **complete** or **partial**.

Types of market failure

- Externalities
- Under-provision of public goods
- Information gaps

Externalities

- An **externality** is a knock-on effect of an economic transaction on a third party.
- Key points of understanding:
  - private marginal cost (PMC) + external marginal cost (EMC) = social marginal cost (SMC)
  - private marginal benefit (PMB) + external marginal benefit (EMB) = social marginal benefit (SMB)
  - social welfare is optimised when SMB = SMC

Key terms

Market failure When the free market leads to a misallocation of resources in an economy.

Complete market failure When the free market fails to create a market for a good or service, also referred to as a missing market.

Partial market failure When a market for a good or service exists, but that good or service is consumed or produced in quantities that do not maximise economic welfare.

Externality A knock-on effect of an economic transaction upon third parties.

Positive externalities in production

- A positive externality is when the actions of firms have wider benefits to society, e.g. building a new airport runway.
- In a free market, individual firms take into account only private costs and private benefits and not those of wider society.
- PMC > SMC, meaning there is a negative external marginal cost.

Positive externalities in consumption

- The actions of individual consumers have wider social benefits, e.g. taking regular exercise and eating healthy food.
- In a free market, individual consumers take into account only their private costs and benefits and not those of wider society.
- As shown in Figure 20, SMB > PMB, meaning there is an external marginal benefit, equal to the vertical distance EG between the SMB and PMB curves at the free market equilibrium quantity, X.

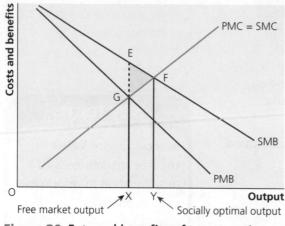

Figure 20 **External benefits of consumption**

- The social optimum quantity occurs where SMB = SMC, i.e. at Y; there is under-consumption of healthy food and exercise equal to Y − X, leading to an overall welfare loss equal to the triangle EFG.

Negative externalities in production

- A negative externality is when the actions of firms have wider social costs, e.g. a coastal oil refinery.
- In a free market, the individual firm takes into account only its private costs and benefits and not those of wider society.
- As shown in Figure 21, SMC > PMC, meaning there is an external marginal cost, equal to the vertical distance BC between the SMC and PMC curves at the free market equilibrium quantity, X.

Key terms

Positive externality A positive knock-on effect of an economic transaction upon third parties, also known as an external benefit.

Private costs The costs to an individual producer involved in a market transaction.

Private benefits The benefits to an individual consumer involved in a market transaction.

Social benefits The total of private benefits plus external benefits of an economic transaction.

Negative externality A negative knock-on effect of an economic transaction upon third parties, also known as an external cost.

Social costs The total of private costs plus external costs of an economic transaction.

Exam tip

Make sure you understand the difference between complete and partial market failure.

Exam tip

The area of welfare loss shown in externality diagrams is also referred to as the area of deadweight loss.

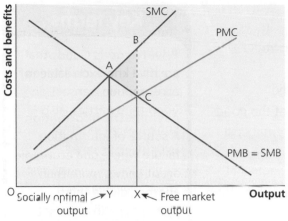

Figure 21 External costs of production

- The social optimum quantity occurs where SMB = SMC, i.e. at Y; there is over-production by the oil refinery equal to X – Y, leading to an overall welfare loss equal to the triangle ABC.

Negative externalities in consumption

- The perceived benefits of consumption activities to individual consumers exceed the benefits to society, e.g. alcohol.
- In a free market, the individual consumer takes into account only their private costs and benefits and not those of wider society.
- PMB > SMB, meaning there is a negative external marginal benefit.

Exam tip

Make sure you can draw accurate diagrams to illustrate positive and negative externalities.

Under-provision of public goods

Key terms

Public goods Goods that are non-excludable and non-rival in consumption.

Non-excludable Where it is not possible to prevent non-paying customers from consuming a good.

Non-rival Where one person's enjoyment of a good does not diminish another person's enjoyment of the good.

Exam tip

Make sure you understand the two key characteristics of public goods.

The free rider problem

- Public goods are an example of complete market failure, as the free market would have no incentive to provide them.
- This is the free-rider problem; individual consumers hope to get a 'free ride' without paying for the benefit they enjoy.

Private goods

- Private goods are the opposite of public goods, i.e. they are excludable and rival.
- Non-payers can be excluded from consuming a good and consumption by one person diminishes the enjoyment of the good by another.

Information gaps

- The free market system is based on the assumption that each economic agent makes rational decisions based on perfect and equal knowledge of the market.
- Asymmetric information is a type of information failure which occurs when one economic agent knows more than another, giving that agent more power in the decision-making process. Examples of asymmetric information:
  - ☐ housing market: estate agents will know more about a property than the buyer
  - ☐ life insurance: the buyer will not reveal all the detrimental aspects of their health
  - ☐ second-hand cars: the seller will know the faults of the car
  - ☐ financial services: a bank may not be fully aware of a customer's ability to repay a loan

Key terms

Private goods Goods that are rival and excludable in consumption.

Asymmetric information A source of information failure where one economic agent knows more than another, giving them more power in a market transaction.

Information failure A source of market failure where market participants do not have enough information to be able to make effective judgements about the 'correct' levels of consumption or production of a good.

Do you know?

1 Define the term 'market failure'.
2 Using a diagram in each case, illustrate positive externalities in consumption and negative externalities in production.
3 State the two key characteristics of a public good.
4 Give three examples of information gaps.

1.4 Government intervention

You need to know

- government intervention in markets
- government failure

Government intervention in markets

Indirect taxes

- Indirect taxes increase the costs of firms: the supply curve shifts leftwards, as shown in Figure 22.

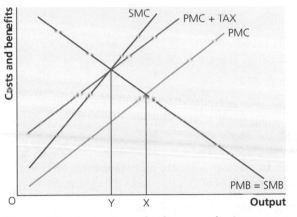

Figure 22 The taxing of a firm producing external costs

- The government can use two different types of indirect tax:
  - □ specific, or unit, taxes — a fixed amount is added per unit of a good or service, e.g. on bottles of alcohol
  - □ ad valorem taxes — these involve adding a percentage of the price of a good or service, e.g. VAT at 20% would add 20p to a product costing £1, but £20 to a product costing £100

Advantages of indirect taxes	Disadvantages of indirect taxes
Revenues for governments can be hypothecated to specific areas of spending	If placed on inelastic goods, the quantity demanded may not fall much unless the tax is very large
Use of the price mechanism leaves it up to consumers and producers to decide how to adjust their behaviour	Difficult to place an accurate value on external costs, which makes it hard to correctly 'internalise' a negative externality
Help to internalise external costs	Tend to be regressive, meaning they take a larger percentage of a poorer person's income
	May reduce international competitiveness of UK firms

Subsidies

- A subsidy is a government grant paid to producers to encourage increased production of certain goods or services.
- They can also be used to promote the use of products that reduce external costs, such as public transport.
- Granting a government subsidy has the effect of shifting the supply curve to the right, as shown in Figure 23.

Key terms

Indirect tax A tax on spending, sometimes used to reduce consumption of demerit goods.

Subsidy A payment made to producers to encourage increased production of a good or service.

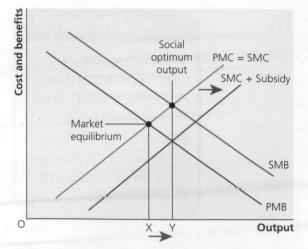

Figure 23 A subsidy to encourage consumption of a product which has external benefits

Advantages of subsidies	Disadvantages of subsidies
Can increase consumption of merit goods	Difficult to place an accurate monetary value on the size of external benefits
Reduce the price of a good, making it more affordable for those on lower incomes, reducing relative poverty	Funding carries an opportunity cost
	Firms may become reliant on subsidies, encouraging productive inefficiency and laziness, reducing international competitiveness
	May be viewed by foreign governments as a form of artificial trade protection, encouraging them to retaliate
	If placed on goods or services with inelastic demand, they may reduce in price but not significantly increase consumption

Maximum prices

- A **maximum price** is a ceiling above which prices are not permitted to rise.
- Free market equilibrium price would be too high for many consumers, leading to problems of reduced affordability, e.g. rent controls to make accommodation more affordable.
- The impact of a maximum price is shown in Figure 24.
- A maximum price (P_{max}) set below the free market price (P_e) for a good creates excess demand, equal to JK in Figure 24.

Key term

Maximum price A price ceiling placed below the free market equilibrium price.

Advantages of maximum prices	Disadvantages of maximum prices
Some people would otherwise not be able to afford certain goods and services, e.g. prescription medications	Creation of excess demand: queues, shortages and waiting lists
Can reduce the ability of firms with monopoly power to exploit consumers through charging higher prices	May lead to black markets for goods and services, e.g. secondary markets for music event tickets

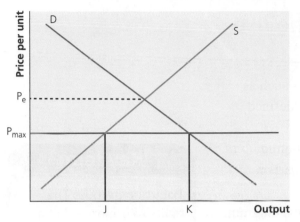

Figure 24 A maximum price set below the equilibrium price

Minimum prices

- A minimum price is a price floor which establishes a legal level below which prices are not allowed to fall, e.g. a national minimum wage.
- The impact of a minimum price is shown in Figure 25.
- A minimum price (P_1) set above the free market price (P^*) for a good will create excess supply, equal to QS–QD in Figure 25.

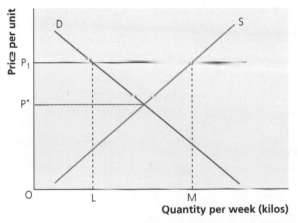

Figure 25 A minimum guaranteed price scheme

Advantages of minimum prices	Disadvantages of minimum prices
Gives producers a guaranteed minimum price and income, which helps to generate a reasonable standard of living	Higher price reduces disposable incomes
	Encourages over-production and inefficiency
Encourages production of essential products, e.g. agriculture	Opportunity costs if governments or other authorities have to purchase excess supplies
	Reduced international competitiveness
Excess supplies may be bought up and stored, to be released in times of future shortage	May encourage people to seek cheaper, potentially more harmful alternatives

Extending property rights and the use of pollution permits

- A key reason for over-exploitation of natural resources such as oceans, forests and the atmosphere is a lack of clearly defined property rights or ownership of these resources.
- **Pollution permits** are legal rights to use or exploit economic resources to a specific degree, e.g. fishing permits or carbon dioxide pollution permits.
- Pollution permits can be presented and analysed using a diagram, as shown in Figure 26.
  - ☐ A regulating organisation such as a government will set a fixed supply of permits, such as S_{2016}, leading to a market price of P_{2016}.
  - ☐ It can reduce supply over time, e.g. to S_{2020}, in order to strengthen incentives for firms to reduce emissions.

> **Key term**
>
> **Pollution permits** The rights to use or exploit an economic resource to a specific degree, e.g. fishing permits or permits to release carbon dioxide into the atmosphere.

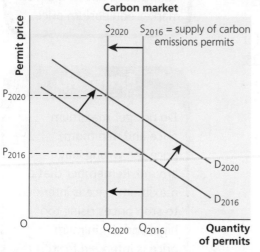

Carbon market

Figure 26 Using pollution permits to tackle environmental market failure

Advantages of pollution permits	Disadvantages of pollution permits
Uses the market mechanism to provide powerful incentives for firms to reduce their carbon emissions	Governments will suffer from imperfect information about the full social costs of carbon dioxide emissions, which may lead to government failure in deciding the quantity of permits to set
Revenues from selling permits can be used to fund 'green' technologies and other environmental schemes	If the price of permits is set too low, firms will not be sufficiently incentivised to cut their carbon dioxide emissions

State provision of public goods

- A government may decide provision cannot be left to the free market, since the good or service may not be provided at all, in the case of public goods.

- The government will organise provision of the product in question, then fund it out of tax revenue.
- Governments may pay a private sector firm to wholly or partially produce the public good.

Correcting information failure

- Governments may intervene in markets where there is too much or too little consumption of particular goods or services, e.g. because of a lack of information about the effects of consumption and production.
- Methods to remedy information failure include:
  - compulsory labelling on food, along with 'traffic-lighting' levels of fat, salt etc.
  - strong health warnings on packs of cigarettes
  - television advertising campaigns discouraging excessive alcohol consumption
- Drawbacks include high costs and a lack of long-term effectiveness.

Regulation

- Examples of **regulation** include:
  - banning smoking in public places
  - imposing maximum emissions levels on new cars
  - setting up regulatory bodies (such as Ofgem) to restrict the activities of dominant firms
- If firms or consumers do not obey the rules and laws, they may be punished, e.g. with fines, limitations on trading activities or even imprisonment.

Key terms

Regulation Rules or laws used to control or restrict the actions of economic agents in order to reduce market failure.

Government failure When government intervention in a market reduces overall economic welfare.

Government failure

- **Government failure** can be defined as when government intervention in a market leads to a misallocation of resources.

The causes of government failure include:

- inadequate information
- unintended consequences
- market distortions
- administrative costs
- regulatory capture

Do you know?

1 Explain two advantages and two disadvantages of using indirect taxation to tackle external costs.

2 Explain two advantages and two disadvantages of using subsidies to encourage consumption of a product that has external benefits.

3 Explain how maximum prices may be used to control the market for rented accommodation.

4 Explain how tradeable pollution permits may be used to reduce external costs.

5 State and explain three possible causes of government failure.

End of section 1 questions

1 Define the term 'positive economic statement'.

2 Define the term 'normal good'.

3 Define the term 'specialisation'.

4 Define the term 'price discrimination'.

5 Define the term 'government failure'.

6 With the help of a PPF diagram, illustrate and explain the opportunity cost situation facing governments with regard to public spending on roads versus schools.

7 With the help of a diagram, explain how an increase in incomes would affect the market for an inferior good.

8 With the help of a diagram, explain how education could lead to positive externalities in consumption in a free market.

2 The UK economy: performance and policies

2.1 Measures of economic performance

You need to know

- how GDP is measured and its uses in indicating living standards and wellbeing
- how inflation is calculated, its causes and consequences
- how unemployment is measured, its causes and consequences
- the components of the balance of payments and how it impacts on other objectives

Economic growth

- Gross domestic product (GDP) measures national income (how much is earned in an economy over time).
- How quickly GDP changes is referred to as the rate of economic growth.
- Prolonged negative economic growth means that the value of GDP is smaller than the previous period — and is sometimes referred to as a recession.
- Growth rates can be compared between countries and also over time.

Real GDP

- Nominal GDP does not distinguish between rises in GDP caused by the following:
  - ☐ actual increases in output produced
  - ☐ higher GDP caused by price increases
- Real GDP shows what GDP can 'buy' after adjusting for changes in prices over time.
- $\text{Real GDP} = \text{nominal GDP} \times \dfrac{\text{price level in previous year}}{\text{price level in current year}}$

Key terms

Gross domestic product (GDP) The value of goods and services produced in the whole economy for a period of time (normally 1 year).

Economic growth The percentage change in GDP over a period of time (normally a quarter of a year or one full year).

Real GDP Value of GDP adjusted for changes in the price level.

- Example: if nominal GDP increases from £2000 to £2200 billion and price level has risen from 114 to 120 over the same period, then:
  - □ real GDP is £2200 billion $\times \dfrac{114}{120} = £2090$ billion
  - □ real economic growth is $\dfrac{£2090bn - £2000bn}{£2000bn} \times 100 = 4.5\%$

Per capita GDP

- Per capita GDP is the average income per person in an economy.
- The formula is:

$$\text{per capita GDP} = \frac{\text{total GDP (in £s)}}{\text{population level}}$$

- A higher GDP per capita increases the population's standard of living.
- GDP can also be expressed in terms of volume and value:
  - □ **volume of output**: quantity of items produced in an economy
  - □ **value of output**: market value of items produced (i.e. volume × selling price)

Other national income measures

- Gross national income (GNI) includes output/income earned by a country's resources, even if located outside the home country.
- National happiness — measures of wellbeing include surveys measuring a population's happiness and adjust economic data to take this into account.
  - □ As incomes rise, we would expect happiness to rise but this is not always closely correlated.
  - □ Income inequality often results in less happiness even if average incomes are rising.
  - □ Surveys used to measure happiness and wellbeing are limited by subjectivity.

Purchasing power parity

- Making comparisons of living standards between countries requires conversion of GDP into common currency.
- Using **purchasing power parity** (PPP) exchange rates avoids the problem of using inappropriate exchange rates, e.g. that are volatile or under- or over-valued.
- The PPP exchange rate is the rate where goods and services in different countries would be the same price once converted into common currencies.

Limitations of using GDP to compare living standards

- Real GDP per capita is used to compare living standards:
  - ☐ between counties
  - ☐ over time
- When comparing countries, PPP exchange rates should be used for comparing data expressed in different currencies.

Comparing living standards between countries and over time

When comparing living standards between countries and over time, other issues include those in the following table.

Synoptic links

Negative externalities are covered in Section 1.3.

Distribution of income	Composition of GDP	Shadow economy	Non-marketed output	Negative externalities	Non-financial factors
Looks at how income is shared out A country with high income inequality has more people with incomes significantly below the average GDP per capita than one with a more equal distribution of income High levels of income inequality make GDP per capita less reliable in measuring living standards	Military spending (which directly benefits few people) can be a significant percentage of GDP Some contributions to GDP —e.g. spending on health and education — increase the living standards more than other contributions	Transactions which are either (or both) illegal and unrecorded Unrecorded transactions add to living standards but do not show in official GDP data Failure to include the shadow economy understates living standards	Only paid-for services are recorded in GDP Services such as DIY and childcare are often not included in the GDP but add to welfare and living standards	Additions to GDP often generate negative externalities Pollution and congestion reduce people's quality of life but increase with economic growth Therefore, increases in GDP often overstate improvements to people's standard of living	Quality and cost of health and education provision Individual freedom Amount of leisure time enjoyed

Inflation

Key terms

Inflation The percentage change in the price level measured over a period of 1 year.

Deflation A fall in the price level measured over a period of time.

Disinflation A fall in the rate of inflation.

Calculating UK inflation using the consumer prices index

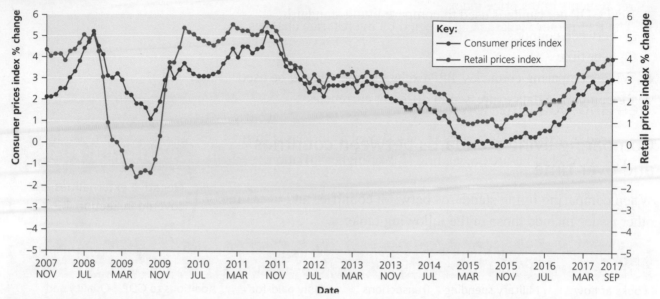

Figure 27 The consumer prices index and retail prices index, all items (% change over 12 months) (Data: ONS)

- The price level, measured by the consumer prices index (CPI), is the average level of prices at a point in time — represented as an index number.
- Inflation is the % change in the CPI, e.g. if it increases from 100 to 103 over one year, the inflation rate is 3%.
- The CPI calculates an average level of prices based on prices for a range of goods and services. This is known as a **basket of goods and services**.
- This basket should represent the spending patterns and prices paid by typical UK households.
- The CPI is a **weighted average**. Goods and services that households spend more of their income on — e.g. food and transport prices — are given a higher weighting.

Limitations of the CPI in measuring the rate of inflation

- It does not include all goods and services.
- It requires updating as spending patterns change, meaning we are not comparing like with like.
- It represents the typical household, making it unlikely to represent individuals entirely accurately.
- It takes no account of improvements to products over time, just their price changes.

Retail prices index

- The retail prices index (RPI) includes the cost of mortgage repayments in the price index.
- The RPI is more volatile and affected by interest rate changes.

Causes of inflation

Demand-pull inflation

- Caused by excessive increases in AD, shown as increases from AD1 to AD4 in Figure 28, leading to ever-higher inflation.

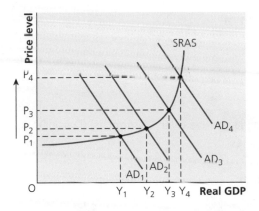

Figure 28 Growth in AD and its impact on demand-pull inflation

- Caused by AD rises that are needed to generate 'full employment' output.
- Demand-pull inflation can be reduced by:
  - ☐ reducing government spending
  - ☐ raising taxes
  - ☐ raising interest rates

Cost-push inflation

- Caused by increases in production costs (i.e. decreases in SRAS or AS) as shown by the leftwards shift from SRAS$_1$ to SRAS$_2$ in Figure 29.

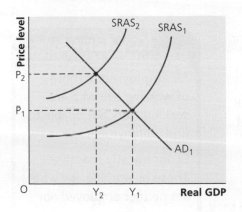

Figure 29 The impact of a leftward shift in SRAS caused by higher costs

- Increases in production costs are caused by:
  - ☐ increases in wages, material costs, power costs
  - ☐ increases in indirect taxes, e.g. VAT
  - ☐ falls in the exchange rates (leading to 'imported inflation')
- Cost-push inflation is accompanied by falling GDP (and rising unemployment).
- Cost-push inflation can be reduced by:
  - ☐ higher interest rates — leading to exchange rate rises
  - ☐ improvements in labour market flexibility, e.g. reduction in trade union power

Growth of the money supply

- Some economists (monetarists) believe all inflation is the result of excessive growth in money supply.

The effects of inflation

Effect name	Explanation
Menu cost	Cost of updating menus, price lists, vending machines etc.
Shoe leather/search costs	Cost in terms of time and money having to research latest prices
Uncompetitive exports	Lower export volumes due to declining international competitiveness
Fiscal drag	People pulled into higher tax bands ending up worse off in real terms
Uncertainty	Harder for businesses to plan ahead — reduced business activity
Policy response	Interest rates are likely to rise to reduce inflation

Employment and unemployment

Measures of unemployment

- Two main measures of unemployment are used in the UK:
  - ☐ **claimant count** includes those receiving benefit payments for being unemployed
  - ☐ the **Labour Force Survey** includes those looking for but unable to find work, whether or not they are receiving benefit payments — this measure is consistent with the international measure of the International Labour Organization (ILO)
- Those of working age are classed as:
  - ☐ economically active — either employed or unemployed
  - ☐ economically inactive — those in full time education, unable to work, retired or choosing to stay at home, e.g. to raise a family

Key terms

Unemployment Those of working age who are seeking work but unable to find employment.

Economically inactive Those of working age who are neither employed nor unemployed.

■ Underemployment is not classed as unemployment — despite the underemployed not being able to work as long as they would choose.

Changes in employment, unemployment and inactivity

Significance of increased employment	Significance of reduced unemployment	Significance of reduced inactivity
Increased incomes	Lower government spending on benefits	Greater potential output
Rising living standards	Less deskilling of population	Less labour shortages
Improved skills of workforce	Closer to full capacity output	Higher tax revenue (if employed)
Higher tax revenue as people work and spend incomes	Reduced social issues, e.g. lower crime, less mental and physical illness	Higher potential spending on welfare/benefits (if unemployed)

Causes (or types) of unemployment

■ **Seasonal unemployment** — caused by decline in demand for seasonal workers.

■ **Cyclical (demand-deficient) unemployment** — caused by insufficient AD, shown in Figure 30 by AD_1 leading to national income of Y_1. This type of unemployment is reduced by increasing AD, through:
  - ☐ lower interest rates
  - ☐ lower taxes
  - ☐ higher government spending

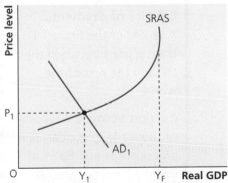

Figure 30 Cyclical unemployment

■ **Frictional unemployment** — caused by people moving into and out of employment — is reduced by:
  - ☐ improving information about job vacancies
  - ☐ ensuring the welfare system does not create incentives to remain unemployed
■ **Structural unemployment** — caused by:
  - ☐ geographical immobility (regional unemployment)
  - ☐ occupational immobility
  - ☐ global factors, e.g. competition from low-cost producers overseas

■ **Real wage inflexibility**

  □ When real wages exceed free market wage rate and cannot
    fall to restore labour market equilibrium. Shown in Figure 31
    where wage rate of W_2 leads to employment level falling to Q_2.

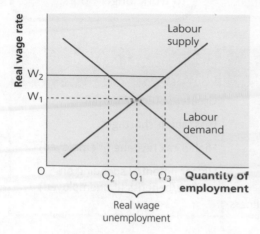

Figure 31 Real wage inflexibility caused by the failure of the labour market to 'clear'

Migration and employment/unemployment

■ **Immigration** affects the domestic labour market:
  □ If immigrants fill vacancies otherwise unfilled, employment
    rate increases.
  □ If immigrants cannot find work or replace others in jobs,
    unemployment rate may increase.

The effects of unemployment

■ Unemployment contributes to:
  □ individual ill-health
  □ family breakdown
  □ higher crime rate (although this is disputed)
■ Unemployment means an economy doesn't operate on its PPF.
■ Unemployment causes a larger budget deficit due to:
  □ higher government expenditure on welfare
  □ less tax revenue collected
■ Long-term unemployment can lead to deskilling of the working
  population (hysteresis).

Balance of payments

■ The balance of payments consists of three components:
  □ current account
  □ capital account
  □ financial account

Key terms

Migration The flow of people into and out of a country seeking employment and residential status.

Immigration The flow of people into a country seeking to stay for the long term (to work/live).

Balance of payments A record of the financial transactions between the UK and the rest of the world.

Current account A record of the trade in goods and services and flows of income between the UK and the rest of the world.

Current account

- Trade in goods: exports of goods minus imports of goods.
- Trade in services: exports of services minus imports of services.
- Balance of trade in goods and services = trade in goods balance + trade in services balance.
- Primary income balance = net investment income flows:
  - □ includes: interest, dividends and profits earned on overseas investments (less the outflows from foreign-owned assets based in the UK)
- Secondary income balance = net transfers of money:
  - □ includes: private transfers between countries — e.g. overseas workers sending wages back to family in home country — foreign aid, grants and gifts

Current account deficits and surpluses

Causes of current account deficits	Causes of current account surpluses
Exchange rate is high	Exchange rate is low
Relative inflation is high	Relative inflation is low
Relative productivity is low	Relative productivity is high
UK economic growth is high	Foreign economic growth is high
Costs of production are rising quickly	Costs of production are low and/or falling

The interconnectedness of economies through international trade

- Economies are interconnected in two ways:
  - □ exports add to AD, to GDP and to job creation
  - □ imports are connected to an economy's GDP level: higher income means more money to spend on imports (remember that one economy's imports are another economy's exports)

Do you know?

1 How is economic growth calculated?
2 Distinguish between deflation and disinflation.
3 Explain why the ILO's measure of unemployment would be higher than the claimant count.

2.2 Aggregate demand

You need to know

- what determines the level of aggregate demand (AD) and the AD curve
- how to distinguish between movements along and shifts of the AD curve
- what determines consumption by households
- what determines investment by businesses
- what determines government expenditure
- what determines net trade (i.e. exports and imports)

The characteristics of AD

The components of **aggregate demand (AD)** are:

- **consumption** (C) by households
- **investment** (I) by businesses
- **government expenditure** (G)
- **net trade**: exports (X) minus imports (M)

The formula is:

$$AD = C + I + G + (X - M)$$

In the UK, the biggest component of AD is consumption, which is almost two-thirds of total AD. Government spending is around a quarter of total AD.

The AD curve

The AD curve shows the relationship between AD (total expenditure) and the price level in an economy. It shifts if any component of AD increases (rightwards shift) or decreases (leftwards shift), as shown in Figure 32.

Key terms

Aggregate demand (AD) Total planned expenditure at any given price level (C + I + G + X − M).

Consumption Spending by households on consumer goods and services.

Investment Spending by businesses on additions to the capital stock of the economy.

Net trade Value of exports less value of imports.

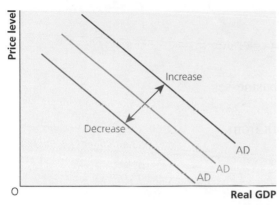

Figure 32 Aggregate demand (AD) showing the amounts of planned expenditure that would occur at different price levels

Consumption (C)

- Consumption rises and falls with increases and decreases in disposable income.
- Disposable income that is not consumed will be saved (and vice versa).
- The link between disposable income, consumption and saving is not always clear as households can finance consumption by borrowing or using past savings.

Other determinants of consumption include interest rates, consumer confidence and the wealth effect.

Interest rates	Consumer confidence	Wealth effect
Higher interest rates encourage saving — and vice versa	The more confident households feel about future prospects, the more they spend on consumption	Higher asset prices — e.g. for houses and shares — increase the wealth of households
Higher interest rates reduce credit-financed consumption — and vice versa	Confident households are more likely to borrow money to finance more consumption	Households increase spending and borrow more against the value of these assets to finance consumption
Higher interest rates mean higher mortgage repayments, meaning less spending — and vice versa		

Investment (I)

Gross and net investment

- Net investment expands an economy's productive capacity by increasing capital stock, e.g. purchase of additional machinery.
- Replacement investment does not add to capital stock but replaces parts of the capital stock that have worn out and need renewing.
- Gross investment includes both net investment and replacement investment.

Rate of economic growth

- Investment is affected by economic growth. This is the accelerator process:
  - ☐ Economic growth should lead to more investment as businesses expand productive capacity.
  - ☐ This allows businesses to produce more output to profit from higher economic growth.

Business expectations and confidence

- Business confidence improves if businesses feel more optimistic about future sales and profits.
- If confidence rises, businesses will invest more, anticipating higher future sales and profits.

Keynes and 'animal spirits'

- The economist Keynes believed investment was determined partly by 'animal spirits' — the beliefs/instincts of managers deciding whether to spend on investment goods.
- The decisions are based on managers' feelings about the future of the economy.
- Often animal spirits move collectively — a herd instinct emerges and investment will significantly rise or fall due to these collective 'spirits'.

Demand for exports

- If businesses can export more, they may need to expand their productive capacity.
- A rise in the demand for exports may increase the amount of investment spending.

Interest rates

- Higher interest rates mean a higher cost of borrowing.
- Higher interest rates reduce the profitability of investment, leading to falls in investment spending (and vice versa).

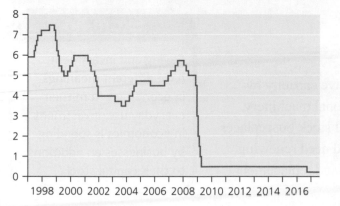

Figure 33 UK interest rates 1997–2017 (Data: ONS)

Access to credit

- Even if interest rates are low, businesses may not be able to borrow money if they can't access credit.
- Banks are sometimes reluctant to lend for business investment purposes, even if businesses are keen to borrow.

Influence of government and regulations

- Governments can influence the level of business investment.
- Changes in tax rates — e.g. corporation tax on business profits — can influence the level of investment spending.
- Governments can give assistance to businesses to encourage investment, e.g. in poorer regions.
- Planning permission rules can be relaxed by the government to encourage more investment in expansion of business premises.

Government expenditure (G)

The trade cycle

The **trade cycle** can be summarised as follows:

- Changes in economic growth affect government expenditure.
  - Lower economic growth usually leads to higher unemployment, requiring more welfare spending (and vice versa).
- Governments often spend more when growth is low to boost AD.

Fiscal policy

- In **fiscal policy**, governments can deliberately change government spending (and taxation) to achieve economic change.
  - Higher government spending increases AD should lead to faster economic growth (and lower unemployment).
  - Lower government spending decreases AD should lead to lower inflation (and lower economic growth).
- Government spending can also generate supply-side improvements.

Net trade (X – M)

- The trade balance, net trade, is the difference between the value of exports of goods and services (X) and the value of imports of goods and services (M).
- The trade balance can be either in balance (where X = M), or:
  - in deficit, where X < M
  - in surplus, where X > M

Main influences on the trade balance

Real income	Exchange rates	State of the world economy	Degree of protectionism	Non-price factors
As UK real incomes rise, spending rises by firms and households Higher UK spending means higher demand for imports, meaning the trade balance moves towards deficit	A rise in the exchange rates will reduce exports due to them being less price competitive in foreign currency terms A rise in the exchange rate will increase imports as they are cheaper in domestic currency terms The effect of exchange rate changes on the trade balance depends on price elasticity of demand for exports and imports	Higher world economic growth leads to higher demand for UK exports (and vice versa) This depends on the size of the economy experiencing growth, e.g. faster growth in Germany is more important for UK exports than faster growth in Belgium	Tariffs, quotas and other forms of protectionism affect UK exports Higher levels of protectionism will lead to lower demand for UK exports	Demand for exports and imports are affected by non-price factors, such as: ■ quality of products ■ reliability of products ■ transport costs

Do you know?

1 State three ways the government could increase the level of AD.

2 Explain how savings and consumption are connected.

3 Explain the link between interest rates and investment.

4 Explain what happens to aggregate demand when the exchange rate rises.

2.3 Aggregate supply

You need to know

■ the differences between the short-run and long-run aggregate supply (AS) curve
■ what determines the AS curve in the short run and long-run
■ the difference between the Keynesian and classical long-run AS curves
■ what shifts the AS curves in both the short run and the long run

The characteristics of AS

The AS curve

■ The aggregate supply (AS) curve is based on the business costs of production.

Key term

Aggregate supply (AS) The total level of output businesses will produce at any given price level.

- The AS curve (Figure 34) usually varies positively with the price level — more is supplied at a higher price level.
- A distinction is made between **short-run AS** and **long-run AS**
  - ☐ short-run AS is upward-sloping
  - ☐ long-run AS curve is vertical

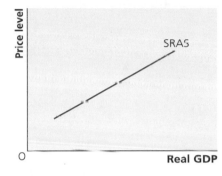

Figure 34 The SRAS curve, showing that as the price level increases, firms will be willing to supply more

Key terms

Short-run AS (SRAS) The level of output supplied by businesses in the short run.

Long-run AS (LRAS) The maximum potential level of output for an economy in the long run.

Movements along and shifts of the AS curve

- Movement along the AS curve happens when the AD curve shifts.

Short-run AS

- The short-run AS (SRAS) curve shows how firms change production decisions given changes in the price level.
- Firms will expand output in the short run when the price level increases (and vice versa).
- The SRAS curve is based on costs of production.

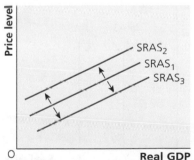

Figure 35 Shifts in the SRAS curve

- If production costs increase, the profitability of production falls. This leads to a decrease in SRAS (leftward shift).
- If production costs fall, the profitability of production increases. This leads to an increase in SRAS (rightward shift).

Factors influencing short-run AS

These include changes in:

- costs of raw material
- wage rates
- energy costs (for power)
- indirect taxes, e.g. VAT
- the exchange rate (affecting import prices)
- worker productivity

Long-run AS

- In the long run, there are different shaped AS curves.
- Both long-run curves are partially vertical.
- The vertical section of the LRAS represents the economy reaching its maximum capacity output level.

The Keynesian AS curve

- An alternative AS curve to the SRAS and LRAS is the Keynesian AS curve (Figure 36).
- At low levels, real GDP can be increased with no upward pressure on prices.
- As an economy gets close to capacity level, prices begin rising — in Figure 36 the AS curve begins to slope upwards.
- The Keynesian AS curve is perfectly inelastic at full capacity output and any increases in AD lead to higher price levels.

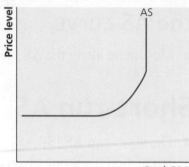

Figure 36 The Keynesian AS curve

Classical AS curve

- The classical AS curve is vertical, meaning any change in AD moves the equilibrium position to a different price level — with no change in the output level.
- A vertical AS curve assumes that, in the long run, output will be always at the full capacity level.
- Increases in full capacity output are achieved through long-run changes to the economy, as shown in Figure 37 by $LRAS_1$ shifting to $LRAS_2$.

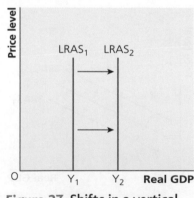

Figure 37 Shifts in a vertical LRAS curve

Shifts in the LRAS curves

- A change in any of the factors influencing the LRAS will shift the curve leftward or rightwards.

Factors influencing long-run AS

Technological advances

- Advances in technology will enable a firm:
  - ☐ to produce more output
  - ☐ to reduce costs of production

Relative productivity

- Productivity measures the rate of production of output.
- A country with higher productivity costs (relative productivity) than others will rise at a slower rate than other countries and it will be able to produce more.

Changes in education and skills

- Improvements in education and skills increase an economy's productive capacity:
  - ☐ improvements in skills level and the quality of education should lead to higher productivity
  - ☐ increased education can reduce occupational immobility

Changes in government regulations

- Investment in infrastructure — e.g. high-speed rail — can increase productive capacity.
- Changes to direct tax levels can change the incentives of workers to supply their labour.
- Changes to welfare benefits can also create incentives for people to work.
- Changes in how governments support businesses — e.g. through grants and tax changes — can generate more business activity.
- Decreases in LRAS may occur if regulations increase costs for business.

Demographic changes and migration

- Increases in the population increase the potential labour supply, increasing LRAS.
- Increases in life expectancy mean people may work longer, increasing LRAS.
- Higher immigration of people of working age will increase LRAS.
- Higher emigration of people of working age will decrease LRAS.
- An ageing population may mean a smaller workforce and reduced LRAS, unless people retire later.

> ### Key term
>
> Emigration The flow of people out of a country seeking to stay in the new country for the long term.

Competition policy

- Increased competition leads to higher output and lower prices — increasing LRAS.
- Governments can encourage competition through policies of **privatisation** and **deregulation**.

Do you know?

1 State three factors that would shift the SRAS to the right.
2 State three factors that would shift the classical AS curve to the right.
3 Explain why the Keynesian AS curve is horizontal at low levels of GDP.

2.4 National income

You need to know

- what is meant by income and wealth for an economy
- how the circular flow of income works
- what macroeconomic equilibrium is
- what the multiplier is — how it is calculated, its effects and its significance

Key terms

Privatisation The transfer of government-owned business enterprises to the private sector.

Regulation The removal of barriers that prevent competition from entering a market.

Circular flow of income A model of the economy showing flows of income and expenditure.

Wealth The value of the stock of assets held.

National income The total income earned in an economy for a period of time.

National income

The circular flow of income

- National income is the same as GDP.
- National income can be measured in three ways:
  - □ adding up all expenditure
  - □ adding up all incomes
  - □ adding up the value of all output produced
- The links between income and expenditure are shown in the circular flow model of the economy:
  - □ money flows from households to firms as expenditure
  - □ money flows back from firms to households as incomes
- The simple circular flow model is shown in Figure 38.

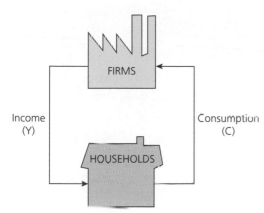

Figure 38 The simple circular flow of income

Income and wealth

- Income is a flow variable — measured over time.
- Wealth is a stock variable — measured at a point in time.
- Income adds to wealth if saved or used to buy assets — e.g. property — which will be held by the owner for some time.
- Wealth falls if asset values decrease — e.g. a stock market crash — or assets are sold and the proceeds spent.

Injections and withdrawals

- The circular flow of income can be updated if we allow for injections and withdrawals into the circular flow.
- The modified circular flow model is shown in Figure 39.

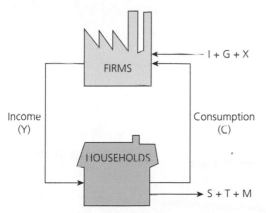

Figure 39 The circular flow with injections for investment (I), government spending (G) and exports (X) plus withdrawals for savings (S), taxation (T) and imports (M)

> ## Key terms
>
> **Injections** Money entering the circular flow from governments, businesses or the foreign sector.
>
> **Withdrawals** Money leaving the circular flow either for savings, taxation or spending on imports.

Equilibrium levels of real national output

Concept of equilibrium real national output

- Macroeconomic equilibrium is reached in two ways:
  - □ injections = withdrawals (in the circular flow of income)
  - □ AD – AS
- At this equilibrium level there is no tendency for the level of real GDP or the price level to change.

AD/AS and macroeconomic equilibrium

Shifts in either the AD or the AS curves will lead to a new macroeconomic equilibrium position.

Increases in AD

- Increases in AD will normally result in either:
  - □ an increase in real GDP
  - □ an increase in the price level
  - □ both of the above
- The closer to its full capacity output level, the more likely it is that an increase in AD will raise prices rather than raise GDP (and vice versa).

Increases in SRAS

- Increases in SRAS will normally result in either:
  - □ an increase in real GDP
  - □ a fall in the price level

Increases in LRAS

- Increases in LRAS will normally result in both rising GDP and a falling price level.

The multiplier

The multiplier ratio

- Extra spending creates incomes for those receiving the spending, which creates further spending, and further income, and so on.
- Changes in spending lead to larger than proportional changes in national income because of the multiplier process

Key term

Multiplier process Where a change in spending leads to a proportionately greater change in income.

The multiplier process

- Extra spending creates extra income, and so on.
- Not all additional income is spent, due to the withdrawals from circular flow.
- Additional income is taxed, saved or spent on imports and is not 'passed on' as extra spending.

Effects of the multiplier on the economy

- Because of the multiplier process, changes in spending result in a change in national income that is greater than the original change in spending.
- The multiplier process can work in both positive (upward) and negative (downward) directions.
- A small change in any component of AD can lead to significant changes to national income.

Marginal propensities and calculation of the multiplier

- The multiplier's size depends on how much of extra income is passed on as extra spending.
- If a higher proportion of income is spent, the size of the multiplier will be bigger.
- The proportion of any additional income that is spent depends on the following:
  □ marginal propensity to tax (MPT)
  □ marginal propensity to import (MPM)
  □ marginal propensity to save (MPS)
- These marginal propensities are normally expressed as a decimal (i.e. 0.1 would be 10% of any additional income).
- The total of the three marginal propensities is called the marginal propensity to withdraw (MPW).
- The size of the multiplier is calculated as follows:

  $1/MPW$ or $1/(1 - MPC)$

- Example:
  □ MPT = 0.2, MPM = 0.1 and MPS = 0.1
  □ Investment expenditure increases by £100 million.
  □ The size of the multiplier is:

  $1/(0.2 + 0.1 + 0.1) = 2.5$

  □ The overall increase in income will be £100 million × 2.5 = £250 million

The significance of the multiplier for shifts in AD

Exam tip

Be careful when calculating the multiplier — look out for fractions and problems with rounding.

■ A change in AD changes national income by a larger amount — both increases and decreases.

■ The multiplier's actual size is uncertain — we can never be sure by how much national income will change when AD changes. For example, if the MPW decreases then the size of the multiplier increases. For example:

☐ if the MPW is 0.25 (i.e. 75% of any additional income is spent), the size of the multiplier would be: $1/0.25 = 4$

☐ if the MPW rises to 0.5, the size of the multiplier falls to: $1/0.5 = 2$

■ A change in government policy may result in an unexpectedly large increase or decrease in national income.

■ The result may have consequences for economic growth, inflation and unemployment.

Do you know?

1 In an economy:

- investment = £35m
- government expenditure = £42m
- taxation = £39m
- exports = £8m
- imports = £12m

If the economy is in equilibrium, what is the level of savings?

2 In an economy, the multiplier has been calculated to be 2.5. If national income rises by £600m, what was the initial change in spending that created the rise in national income?

3 In an economy, MPT = 0.15, MPS = 0.15 and MPM = 0.3. If investment rises by £45m, what impact would this have on national income?

2.5 Economic growth

You need to know

■ what factors cause economic growth
■ the differences between actual and potential growth
■ what the trade cycle is
■ the characteristics of booms and recessions
■ what output gaps are and how they are caused
■ the costs and benefits of growth

Causes of growth

Factors that could cause economic growth

- Economic growth is caused by:
  - ☐ increases in AD (as long as the economy isn't already at full capacity level)
  - ☐ increases in AS

Increases in AD come from any of the following.

- Increases in consumption, caused by:
  - ☐ lower interest rates
  - ☐ lower taxes on incomes
  - ☐ higher consumer confidence
  - ☐ greater availability of consumer credit

- Increases in investment, caused by:
  - ☐ lower interest rates
  - ☐ faster economic growth (the accelerator effect)
  - ☐ lower taxes on profits
  - ☐ advances in technology
  - ☐ higher business confidence

- Increases in government expenditure, caused by:
  - ☐ expansionary fiscal policy (deliberately increasing government spending)
  - ☐ automatic stabilisers

- Increases in net exports, caused by:
  - ☐ a fall in the exchange rate
  - ☐ reduced trade barriers
  - ☐ improvements in the competitiveness of export industries

Increases in AS come from supply-side factors — dealt with in Section 2.6.

The distinction between actual and potential growth

Differences between actual growth and potential growth are summarised in the following table.

Actual growth	Potential growth
Caused by increases in AD	Caused by increases in economy's productive capacity (shown by shift to right in LRAS or PPC)
Can be achieved through changes in government policy	
Measured by percentage increase in real GDP over time	Future actual growth is made possible by increases in potential growth
Caused by increases in any component of SRAS	Estimates of UK long-run growth are between 2% and 2.5% per year
Shown in Figure 40 as a move from A to B	Shown in Figure 40 as a move from B to C

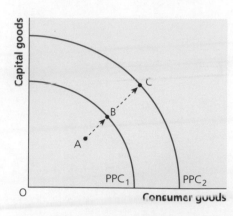

Figure 40 Short-run and long-run economic growth

Key terms

Actual growth Growth in real GDP caused by increased utilisation of unemployed factors (also known as short-term growth).

Potential growth Growth caused by an expansion of an economy's productive capacity (also known as long-term growth).

The importance of international trade for (export-led) economic growth

- Increases in exports (falls in imports) increase AD.
- Improvements in net exports generate actual growth.
- Improvements in net exports also help the current account balance on balance of payments.
- Improvements in export levels also have multiplier effects on the economy.

Synoptic link

There is a link between actual and potential growth and the factors that affect the shape of the PPF and the position within (or on) the PPF covered in Section 1.1.

Output gaps

Distinction between actual and long-term trends in growth rates

- Growth in potential output means the economy can produce more.
- If actual growth is lower than potential growth for long periods, potential growth may fall.

Positive and negative output gaps

- Actual growth diverges from potential growth resulting in output gaps, as shown in Figure 41 as positive or negative

Key term

Output gaps The different between actual output and potential output.

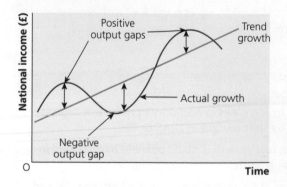

Figure 41 Output gaps exist when short-run growth deviates from long-run or trend growth

- Positive output gap: actual growth > potential growth
  - □ unemployment probably falling
  - □ inflation probably rising
- Negative output gap: actual growth < potential growth
  - □ unemployment probably rising
  - □ inflation probably falling

Use of an AD/AS diagram to illustrate output gaps

- Output gaps can show the level of spare capacity in an economy.
- Output gaps can also be shown using AD/AS diagrams:
  - □ negative output gaps: when AD is lower than the level needed to generate full capacity output
  - □ positive output gaps: when AD is higher than the level needed to generate full capacity output (and is likely to lead to higher inflation)

Trade (business) cycle
Understanding the trade (business) cycle

- Actual growth varies in a repeated, cyclical pattern — the trade (business) cycle.

- The four stages of the trade cycle (Figure 42) are:
  - □ boom
  - □ downturn
  - □ recession
  - □ recovery

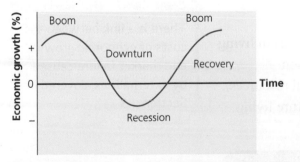

Figure 42 The trade (or business or economic) cycle

Key terms

Trade (business) cycle The repeated fluctuations in actual growth over time.

Boom The period where actual growth is above average (and above the potential growth rate).

Recession The period where actual growth is negative for two consecutive quarters.

Characteristics of booms and recessions

Features of a boom	Features of a recession
Above average economic growth	Economic growth is very low or negative
Unemployment falls, reaching low levels	Unemployment rises quickly, reaching high levels
Inflation rises as economy 'overheats'	Inflation falls, reaching low levels (with possible deflation)
High consumer/business confidence	Low consumer/business confidence
Budget balance moves into surplus/smaller deficit	Budget balance moves further into deficit
Current account balance moves into deficit/deficit increases	Current account balance moves towards/into surplus

The impact of economic growth

Benefits of economic growth include:	Costs of economic growth include:
Higher living standards for consumers	Increases in negative externalities
Easier to find jobs for unemployed people	Potential increases in inequality
Social indicator improvements — good for consumers	Natural resource depletion
Increased tax revenue for government	Increases in inflation
Lower welfare expenditure for government	Worsening current account balance
Lower absolute poverty	
Status and prestige for the government	

Growth and living standards

- Growth should raise current living standards.
- Growth may lead to inflation, leading to future decreases in living standards when the government tries to control inflation.
- If the growth is unsustainable (i.e. by depleting natural resources), it improves current living standards but may mean future living standards are lower.

Synoptic link

There is a link between the costs of economic growth and market failure caused by externalities, covered in Section 1.3.

Do you know?

1 State three factors that would lead to higher potential growth.
2 State three features of a recession.
3 Explain two reasons why economic growth can have negative effects.

2.6 Macroeconomic objectives and policies

You need to know

- the government's macroeconomic objectives
- how monetary and fiscal policies can be used to affect the economy's demand-side
- how supply-side policies affect the economy's supply-side
- how policies conflict with each other and how this makes it difficult to achieve multiple objectives

Possible macroeconomic objectives

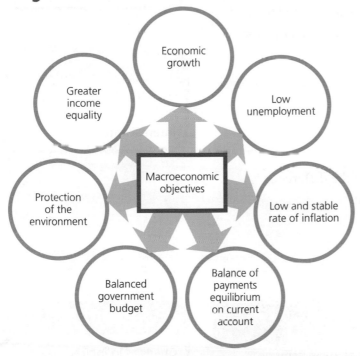

Demand-side policies

Distinction between monetary and fiscal policy

- Monetary policy is the use of interest rates, control of the money supply and the availability of credit to achieve macroeconomic objectives.
- Fiscal policy is the change to government expenditure and rates of taxation to achieve macroeconomic objectives.

Monetary policy instruments

Interest rates

- Interest rates are set by the Monetary Policy Committee (MPC) of the Bank of England.
- These are used to affect AD (mainly through changes to consumption (C) and investment (I)):
  - ☐ increases in interest rates will lower AD
  - ☐ decreases in interest rates will increase AD

Asset purchases to increase the money supply (quantitative easing)

- Low interest rates do not always boost AD sufficiently and the Bank of England can use quantitative easing.
- The Bank of England creates more money electronically, which is used to buy bonds from the financial sector, which then increases the price of bonds and lowers interest rates.
- Commercial banks now have more money available to lend and, given the low interest rates, there should be more demand for borrowing from the private sector.

> ### Key term
>
> **Quantitative easing** This is where the central bank purchases financial assets specifically to inject new money into the economy to stimulate activity.

Fiscal policy instruments

- Changes in government spending (G)
- Changes in taxation (T)
- The government's budget (fiscal) balance is the difference between government spending and taxation:
  - ☐ budget deficit: G > T
  - ☐ budget surplus: G < T

> ### Exam tip
>
> Monetary policy is enacted mainly through changes in interest rates.

Types of taxation

Direct taxes are placed on incomes	Indirect taxes are placed on expenditure
Income tax — paid on wages and salaries	VAT — paid on most items of expenditure
Corporation tax — paid on company profits	Excise duties — paid on various items, such as tobacco, alcohol and fuel
Capital gains tax — paid on the profits made from trade in assets	Customs duties — paid on some imports
Inheritance tax — paid on inherited income	

> ### Exam tip
>
> Changes in indirect tax rates are likely to affect aggregate supply rather than aggregate demand (though the economy will move along the AD curve).

Supply-side policies

Supply-side policies are those designed to boost the productive capacity of the economy. They fall into two main categories, market based and interventionist.

Market-based policies

- Cutting corporation tax
- Removing regulations
- Privatisation and deregulation
- Lower income tax — to encourage labour supply

Interventionist policies

- Improved education — to boost productivity and reduce labour immobility.
- Improved infrastructure — to attract businesses and boost labour mobility.

Supply-side policies and AD/AS

- Supply-side policies (if successful) boost the productive capacity.
- Increases in productive capacity are shown by increases in AS (LRAS and Keynesian AS curves).
- Figure 43 shows that if supply-side policies are successfully implemented, AD can expand without generating price increases.

Strengths and weaknesses of supply-side policies

Strengths	Weaknesses
Avoid conflicts with other objectives	Tax cuts often favour high earners
Increase productive capacity of economy	Welfare cuts fall disproportionately on lower income earners
Lower unemployment	Relative poverty is increased
Not expensive (for market-based policies)	Very long time lag with most policies
Reduce economically inactive population	Investment in infrastructure is expensive

Policies and AD/AS diagrams

Policies to increase AD include:

- lower taxes
- higher government spending
- lower interest rates

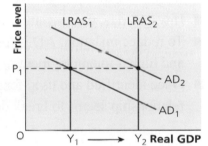

Figure 43 Impact of successful supply-side policies

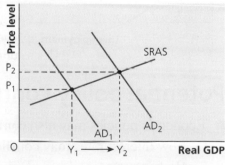

Figure 44 Increases in AD will produce short-run growth in the economy

Conflicts and trade-offs between objectives and policies

Potential conflicts and trade-offs between macroeconomic objectives

Potential policy conflicts and trade-offs between the macroeconomic objectives include:

- both low unemployment and low inflation
- economic growth and low inflation
- economic growth and achieving balance on the current account
- low unemployment and achieving balance on the current account
- supply-side increases achieving an equitable distribution of income

Short-run Phillips curve

- A low rate of inflation moves along the short-run Phillips curve (SRPC) leftwards but only to a higher rate of inflation.
- As unemployment falls, trade unions have more power to push up wages — especially as labour shortages emerge.
- If wages rise, then inflation will also rise — the trade-off.
- To reduce inflation, AD is reduced, and this leads to lower GDP and higher unemployment.
- Once identified and used for policy purposes, the SRPC relationship seems to break down.

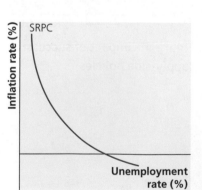

Figure 45 The short-run Phillips curve, showing the trade-off between unemployment and inflation

Potential policy conflicts and trade-offs

- Economic policies may also conflict with each other:
  - ☐ Low interest rates may conflict with expansionary fiscal policy.
  - ☐ High interest rates may conflict with contractionary fiscal policy.

Synoptic link

Trade-offs and policy conflicts illustrate the basic economic concept of opportunity cost.

Key terms

Policy conflicts Where using a policy to achieve one objective moves further away from achieving another objective.

Trade-offs Improvements in achieving one objective mean moving further away from achieving another objective.

Short-run Phillips curve (SRPC) Shows an apparent inverse relationship between the rate of inflation and the rate of unemployment.

☐ Supply-side policies may conflict with expansionary fiscal policy.

☐ Contractionary fiscal policy may conflict with (interventionist) supply-side policies.

■ As a result, we often refer to the overall 'stance of policies' — that is the overall combined effect of fiscal, monetary and supply-side policies — as being 'loose' (expansionary) or 'tight' (contractionary).

Do you know?

1 Explain why the short-run Phillips curve appears as it does.

2 Explain why a supply-side policy can also be a fiscal policy.

3 Explain why policies may conflict with aiming for an equitable distribution of income.

End of section 2 questions

Short questions

1 Define the term 'long-run aggregate supply'.

2 Define the term 'frictional unemployment'.

3 In an economy, exports rise by $25 billion. MPT = 0.25, MPS = 0.05 and MPM = 0.2. Calculate the change in national income that will follow.

4 Define the term 'contractionary monetary policy'.

Longer questions

1 Assess the consequences of high economic growth on an economy.   (9 marks)

2 Discuss the effectiveness of methods used by a government to reduce the natural rate of unemployment.   (15 marks)

Essay-style questions

1 To what extent is the GDP of an economy a good indicator of the living standards of its population?   (25 marks)

2 To what extent do attempts to lower the unemployment rate conflict with a government's ability to achieve other macroeconomic objectives?   (25 marks)

3 Business behaviour and the labour market

3.1 Business growth

You need to know
- sizes and types of firms
- business growth
- demergers

Sizes and types of firms

Reasons some firms stay small	Reasons some firms choose to grow
Operating in a niche market	Economies of scale
Lack of economies of scale	Increased market share
Avoiding diseconomies of scale	Economies of scope
Focus on customer service	Managers' objectives

The divorce of ownership from control

Separation of ownership from control may lead to conflicting objectives, with directors pursuing their own objectives and with profit maximisation, the assumed shareholder objective, not being a top priority. This is known as the **principal-agent problem**.

Public sector, private sector and not-for-profit organisations

- **Private sector firms** aim to make a profit.
- **Public sector firms** have objectives other than profit.
- **Not-for-profit organisations** are private sector firms whose primary objective is not profit, although they generally have to cover their costs.

Key terms

Firm A production unit.

Niche market A smaller segment of a large market.

Principal-agent problem When the objectives of a firm's owners and managers diverge.

Business growth

Organic growth

- Where firms grow from within, e.g. by buying new machines or employing more workers.
- The easiest, but possibly the slowest, form of growth.

External growth

- Where firms grow by merging with or buying other firms.

Horizontal integration

Where firms at the same stage of production merge.

Advantages	Disadvantages
Economies of scale	Focus on a limited product range
Increased market share	Diseconomies of scale
Eliminates competition	Duplication of resources
Reduced risk of takeover	Possible redundancies

Backward vertical integration

Where a firm buys another firm which is closer to the raw material stage of production.

Advantages	Disadvantages
Control over supply of raw materials	Firm may not need all supplies
May prevent other firms getting supplies	Lack of specialist knowledge
Increased profit through less 'middle-men'	

Forward vertical integration

Where a firm buys another firm which is closer to the sales stage of production.

Advantages	Disadvantages
Control over selling	Firm may not offer enough choice for consumers
More effective market research	Possible lack of sales and marketing expertise

Conglomerate integration

- Also called diversification or lateral integration.
- Where a firm buys another firm in an unrelated industry.

Advantages	Disadvantages
Spreads risk	Possible lack of expertise in new areas
Different products support others at different stages of business cycle	Brands may become diluted
Better brand recognition	

Constraints on business growth

- Market size
- Access to finance
- Objectives of owners
- Government regulation

Demergers

Where a firm sells off part of its operations, e.g. to raise finance or to focus on its core business.

Do you know?

1 Explain why some firms may choose to remain small.
2 Explain the principal-agent problem.
3 State three ways businesses may grow externally.
4 Identify two advantages and two disadvantages of each form of business growth.

3.2 Business objectives

You need to know

- profit maximisation
- revenue maximisation
- sales maximisation
- satisficing

- When a firm undertakes production, it turns inputs of factors of production (which generate costs) into outputs of goods and services (which generate revenues), as shown in Figure 46.

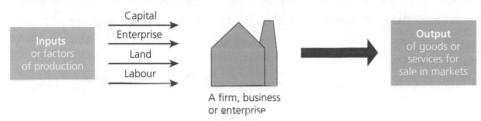

Figure 46 A firm undertaking production

Profit maximisation

- The main objective of firms is maximising profit, i.e. making the maximum positive difference between costs and revenues.
- Making large profits enables firms to:
  - □ re-invest funds into developing new products, leading them to gain more customers
  - □ pay out higher returns to shareholders, which may encourage more people to buy shares in the company or help boost the share price
- Maximum profit occurs when a firm's total revenue (TR) exceeds total costs (TC) by the greatest amount.
- The profit-maximising rule for firms in all market structures is the level of output where marginal cost (MC) = marginal revenue (MR).
- As shown in Figure 47, as MC meets MR from below, at output M_1, profit is maximised.

Key term

Average revenue (AR) Total revenue divided by quantity sold. Equal to price, in a firm that sells one product at a fixed price.

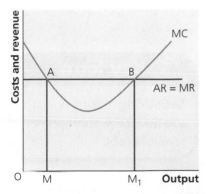

Figure 47 The profit-maximising rule for a firm in perfect competition

- While MC is also equal to MR at output M, crucially this is the profit minimisation or loss maximisation level of output, as the cost of every unit of output up to this point has exceeded the addition to total revenue.
- Between output M and M_1, the addition to total revenue exceeds the addition to total cost.

Exam tip

Note that the profit-maximising rule for every firm in each type of market structure is MC = MR.

Revenue maximisation

- An alternative to profit maximisation.
- The firm cuts price to the point where extra revenue from selling another unit is balanced by reduced price on every item it is currently selling.
- Occurs where marginal revenue is zero (MR = 0).
- May be a key objective if managers are paid according to how much is sold.

Exam tip

Don't confuse profit maximisation with revenue maximisation.

Sales maximisation

- When a firm sells as much as possible, subject to making at least normal profit.
- Can be used to prevent new entry.
- Occurs where AC = AR, as shown in Figure 48.

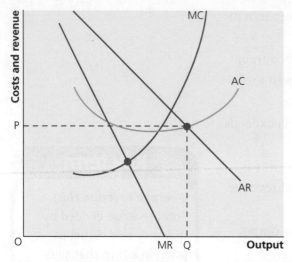

Figure 48 Sales maximisation occurs at Q where AC = AR

Satisficing

- Some firms will aim to make just enough profit to keep shareholders happy — a strategy called **satisficing**.
- This objective recognises that it is difficult, in practice, to identify the level of output necessary to maximise profit.

Key term

Satisficing Making do with a satisfactory, sub-optimal level of profit.

Do you know?

1 State three objectives of firms.
2 Explain why rational firms seek to maximise profit.
3 Explain the objective of revenue maximisation.
4 Explain why firms may have to satisfice.

3.3 Revenues, costs and profits

You need to know
- revenue
- costs in the short run and in the long run
- economies and diseconomies of scale
- normal profits, supernormal profits and losses

Revenue

- Total revenue (TR) is found by multiplying price (P) by quantity sold (or demanded) (Q):

  $$TR = P \times Q$$

- To calculate **average revenue (AR)**, total revenue (TR) is divided by the quantity sold (Q):

  $$AR = \frac{TR}{Q}$$

  - average revenue is the same as price
  - average revenue shows the quantity demanded at each price: the demand curve is also the average revenue curve
- Marginal revenue (MR) is the addition to a firm's total revenue from selling an additional unit of output.

Key terms

Total revenue (TR) The money a firm receives from selling its output, calculated by price × quantity sold.

Marginal revenue (MR) The addition to a firm's total revenue from selling an additional unit of output.

Price elasticity of demand (PED) and its relationship to revenue

- PED was covered in Section 1.2.
- The mid-point on a straight line has unitary elasticity and MR = 0.

■ We can draw TR, AR and MR on a graph (Figure 49): when MR is positive PED is elastic, and when MR is negative PED is inelastic.

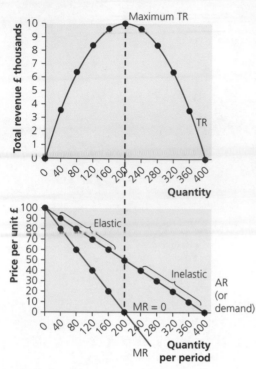

Figure 49 A graphical representation of the relationship between TR, AR and MR

Costs

Significance of the short run versus the long run

■ The **short run** is when at least one factor of production is fixed in quantity.

■ The **long run** is the period of time over which a firm can vary all of the factors of production and may increase or reduce its scale.

Fixed costs

■ **Fixed costs** do not vary directly with output in the short run, e.g. rents on business premises.

■ Average fixed costs (AFC), however, fall as output increases, as the firm is able to spread the fixed costs over an increasing volume of output, as shown in Figure 50.

■ The formula is: $\text{AFC} = \dfrac{\text{total fixed costs}}{\text{output}}$

Variable costs

■ **Variable costs** are those that vary directly with the level of output, e.g. raw materials.

■ As shown in Figure 50, average variable costs (AVC) initially fall in the short run but begin to rise at higher levels of output.

■ The formula is: $\text{AVC} = \dfrac{\text{total variable costs}}{\text{output}}$

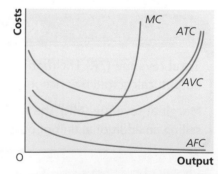

Figure 50 Short-run cost curves

Total costs

- **Total costs** are made up of total fixed costs and total variable costs.
- Total costs (TC) = total fixed costs (TFC) + total variable costs (TVC).
- **Average (total) costs**, or costs per unit of output, are found by dividing total costs by total output.

  So: $\text{ATC} = \dfrac{\text{total costs (TC)}}{\text{total output}}$

- Average total costs (ATC) = average fixed costs (AFC) + average variable costs (AVC), as shown in Figure 50.

Marginal costs

- This is the addition to a firm's total costs from making an additional unit of output.
- As increasing units of variable factors of production are added to a fixed factor in the short run, the **marginal cost** of production initially declines and then begins to rise.
- The shape of the marginal cost curve, along with all short-run cost curves, is shown in Figure 50.

Derivation of short-run cost curves from the assumption of diminishing marginal productivity

The law of diminishing returns

- In the short run costs may be influenced by **the law of diminishing returns**.
- When additional units of variable factors of production are added to a fixed factor, marginal product (MP) will rise at first and then eventually decrease.
- Figure 51 shows the law of diminishing returns as additional units of labour are added to a fixed factor, e.g. land or capital.

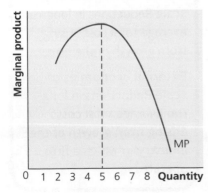

Figure 51 Marginal product increases and eventually decreases as diminishing returns sets in

Economies and diseconomies of scale

Economies of scale

- The benefits of a firm increasing its output, leading to reduced average total costs.
- As a firm increases its output from 0 to Q in the long run, average costs begin to fall up to output Q_1 (Figure 52), due to the effect of one or more **economies of scale**.

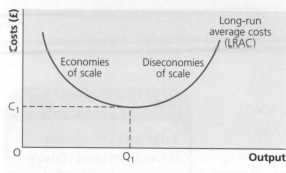

Figure 52 Long-run average costs curve

Diseconomies of scale

- When an increase in a firm's output leads to an increase in average costs of production — see Figure 52 (output levels beyond Q_1).
- Possible sources of **diseconomies of scale** include problems with:
  - □ coordination and control
  - □ communication
  - □ slowness
  - □ x-inefficiency

Internal and external economies of scale

- Internal economies of scale come about as a result of the growth of the firm itself and include:
  - □ **Financial economies of scale**: The larger and more reputable a firm is, the more likely it is that it will be offered cheaper finance.
  - □ **Technical economies of scale**: Larger firms can generally afford the latest specialist equipment, which can make them more efficient, reducing average costs.
  - □ **Marketing economies of scale**: Larger firms can spread large advertising budgets over a greater range of output.
  - □ **Managerial economies of scale**: Larger firms can afford to recruit the highest profile CEOs, who may be able to significantly cut the firm's costs.
  - □ **Commercial economies**: Discounts for buying in bulk.
- External economies of scale occur when firms benefit from the growth of the industry in which they operate.

Key terms

Economies of scale The reduced average total costs that firms experience by increasing output in the long run.

Diseconomies of scale Increases in average total costs that firms may experience by increasing output in the long run.

Internal economies of scale Reductions in long-run average total cost arising from growth of the firm.

External economies of scale Reductions in long-run average total costs arising from growth of the industry in which a firm operates.

Minimum efficient scale

- The lowest level of output at which average total costs of production are minimised.
- In Figure 52, the minimum efficient scale occurs at output Q_1.
- In industries where the **minimum efficient scale (MES)** of production occurs at a large scale of output, only large firms will be able to achieve this. This can be a significant **barrier to entry**, leading to the dominance of one or a small number of powerful firms.

Exam tips

- You should understand the significance of the minimum efficient scale for the structure of an industry and barriers to entry.
- The concept of the minimum efficient scale may be used as an argument in favour of large, dominant firms, since firms may need to be large to achieve maximum economies of scale.

Normal profits, supernormal profits and losses

- **Profit** is the difference between total revenue and total costs, i.e. Total profit = total revenue − total costs.
- If this figure is negative, a **loss** is made.
- Profit creates an incentive for entrepreneurs to take a business risk.
- **Normal profit** is the level of profit required to reward the entrepreneur for taking a risk.
- **Supernormal profit** is profit greater than normal profit, sometimes referred to as excess profit.
- A loss occurs when a firm's total costs exceed total revenue, or average cost is greater than price per unit.
- Break-even occurs when TC = TR or AC = AR, and the firm will stay in business because it is earning normal profit.
- If a firm is covering its average variable costs, it will stay in business.
- So in Figure 53, the point where P = AVC and any price below that is the point at which it will shut down.

Key terms

Minimum efficient scale (MES) The lowest level of output at which average total costs of production are minimised.

Barrier to entry Any feature of a market that makes it difficult or impossible for new firms to enter.

Profit The difference between total revenue and total costs.

Loss If the difference between total revenue and total costs is negative, a loss is made.

Normal profit The minimum level of profit required to reward the entrepreneur for taking a risk and therefore to stay in a particular line of business.

Supernormal profit Profit over and above normal profit, sometimes referred to as abnormal or excess profit.

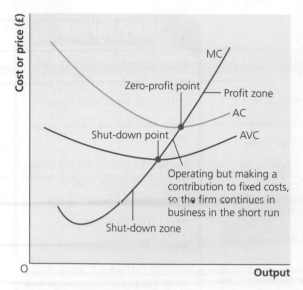

Figure 53 Break-even and shut-down points on the average cost diagram

Do you know?

1 Using a diagram, explain the relationship between marginal revenue and price elasticity of demand.

2 Use a diagram to illustrate the shape of a firm's short-run cost curves.

3 Explain the law of diminishing returns.

4 Explain any two economies of scale.

5 Explain the conditions under which a firm would shut down in the short run.

3.4 Market structures

You need to know

■ efficiency
■ perfect competition and monopolistic competition
■ oligopoly and monopoly
■ monopsony
■ contestability

Efficiency

■ Efficiency measures how well economic resources are used.

■ **Allocative efficiency** occurs where price equals marginal cost (P = MC), as shown in Figure 54.

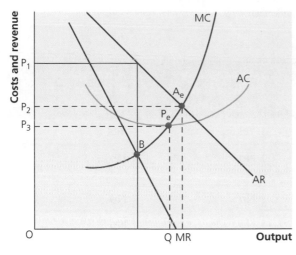

Figure 54 The relative prices and outputs of productive efficiency P_e and allocative efficiency A_e

- Allocative efficiency means that consumers are paying the exact amount it costs to produce the last unit of output.
- **Productive efficiency** is where a firm operates at minimum average cost.
- Productive efficiency occurs where MC = AC, as shown in Figure 54.
- **Dynamic efficiency** refers to efficiency over time.
- Dynamic efficiency can be achieved by, for example, innovating or investing in human capital.
- **X-inefficiency** refers to a lack of dynamism when firms have little or no competition.
- X-inefficiency leads to average costs being higher than in a competitive market, as shown in Figure 55.

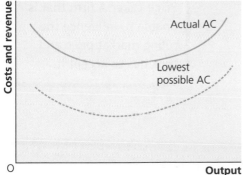

Figure 55 X-inefficiency

Efficiency in different market structures

- Market structure refers to the number and size of firms within a market for a particular good or service and the extent to which they compete with one another.
- Some markets are supplied by a large number of small firms, e.g. commodities such as wheat.

■ Other markets are supplied by one firm, or a small number of firms, e.g. internet search engines such as Google.

Market structure	Productively efficient in the short run?	Productively efficient in the long run?	Allocatively efficient in the short run?	Allocatively efficient in the long run?
Perfect competition	No	Yes	Yes	Yes
Monopolistic competition	No	No	No	No
Oligopoly	No	No	No	No
Monopoly	No	No	No	No

The spectrum of competition

■ The spectrum of competition ranges from perfect competition at one end to pure monopoly at the other end, with anything between qualifying as imperfect competition.

■ Perfect competition is the most competitive form of market structure.

■ Pure monopoly exists when only one firm supplies the market and is the least competitive form of market.

Perfect competition

Characteristics of perfect competition:

■ a large number of buyers and sellers

■ no firm is large enough to influence the market price — each is a price taker

■ perfect knowledge of the market

■ no barriers to entry to or exit from the market

■ each firm sells an identical product

Perfect competition in the short run

■ Firms in perfect competition face a perfectly elastic demand curve, as shown in Figure 56.

■ A constant price means that both average revenue (AR) and marginal revenue (MR) are constant.

■ Supply and demand analysis (Figure 56) shows how perfect competition works.

Key terms

Perfect competition A market structure that has a large number of buyers and sellers who have perfect information about the market, identical products and few, if any, barriers to entry.

Pure monopoly When only one firm supplies the market.

Imperfect competition Any market structure that is not perfect competition.

Price taker A firm that is unable to influence the ruling market price and thus has to accept it.

- Figure 56(a) shows a highly competitive market, with firms supplying this market earning supernormal profits. In Figure 56(b), initial market equilibrium price is P_1 and market output is Q_1.
- If other firms become aware that the existing firms in the market are earning supernormal profits, they will enter the market easily due to the low barriers to entry.

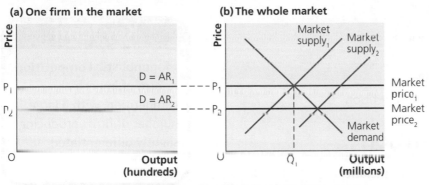

Figure 56 **Price determination in highly competitive markets**

- This will have the effect of increasing overall supply in the market, as shown in Figure 56(b), which leads to a rightward shift of the market supply curve.
- This reduces the equilibrium price to P_2 as output increases beyond Q_1.
- This increase in supply and reduction in price will occur up to the point at which only normal profit is made, meaning that only the most competitive firms survive in the market.
- In the short run it is possible for a firm to be making a loss, normal profit or supernormal profit. The latter case is shown in Figure 57.

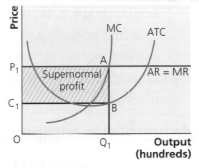

Figure 57 **Short-run profit maximisation under perfect competition**

Perfect competition in the long run

- Perfectly competitive firms make normal profit in the long run only.
- Any supernormal profit encourages firms to enter the industry, increasing market supply, while firms making losses will leave the market in the long run.
- Only firms making normal profit remain in the market, illustrated in Figure 58, with individual firms producing at the profit-maximising output Q_1 and price P_1.

- Long term, firms in perfect competition are both productively efficient and allocatively efficient.

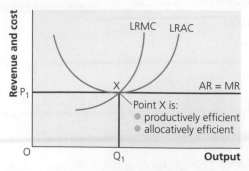

Figure 58 Static efficiency in perfect competition

Monopolistic competition

- Features of monopolistic competition include:
  - □ large number of producers
  - □ similar products are differentiated from one another, e.g. by branding or quality
  - □ low barriers to entry and exit
- Examples include independent fast-food takeaways, plumbers and hairdressers.

Monopolistic competition in the short run

- The short-run profit-maximising situation facing a firm in monopolistic competition is like that of the monopolist, with some brand loyalty leading to a downward-sloping demand curve, as shown in Figure 59.

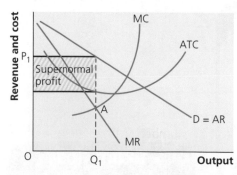

Figure 59 A firm in monopolistic competition in the short run

- Firms maximise profit where MC = MR, at output Q_1, leading to an equilibrium price of P_1.
- Firms can make supernormal profit equal to the shaded area.

Monopolistic competition in the long run

- Firms make only normal profit.
- Low barriers to entry mean new firms can enter the industry relatively easily, attracted by supernormal profits made by some firms.

Key term

Monopolistic competition
A form of imperfect competition, with a large number of firms producing slightly differentiated products.

Exam tip

Don't confuse monopolistic competition with monopoly. The characteristics of monopolistic competition place it closer to perfect competition than monopoly in terms of market structure.

Exam tip

Remember that the profit-maximising level of output for all forms of market structure occurs where MC = MR.

- This reduces demand (D = AR) for the individual firm as new entrants take some market share.
- Ultimately, the D = AR curve is just tangential to the firm's ATC curve, meaning normal profit is made at the profit-maximising output Q_1.
- Figure 60 illustrates a firm in monopolistic competition in the long run.

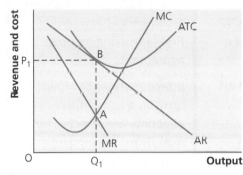

Figure 60 A firm in monopolistic competition in the long run

Oligopoly

- An **oligopoly** is where a small number of relatively powerful firms compete for market share.
- Markets tend to be highly concentrated.
- Firms are interdependent.

Concentration ratio

- The **concentration ratio** is the total market share held by the largest firms in the industry.

Game theory

- The study of strategies used to make decisions.
- Can be used to analyse the actions of firms in oligopoly.

Pricing strategies

- **Price wars**: when price cutting leads to retaliation by other firms.
- **Predatory pricing**: cutting prices below average costs to force other firms out of the market.
- **Limit pricing**: cutting prices below the level new entrants would require to cover their costs.
- **Price leadership**: the dominant firm sets prices that other firms follow.
- **Non-price competition**: competing on factors other than price, e.g. product differentiation or loyalty cards.

Collusive and non-collusive behaviour

- Collusion occurs when firms work together to determine price and/or output.
- This reduces uncertainty that may exist among firms in the industry regarding pricing and output decisions of rivals.
- Collusion between firms can be either tacit or overt.
- Tacit collusion is where firms appear to be organising prices and/or output between themselves without a formal agreement having been made, whereas overt collusion involves a more formal, open agreement.
- In making collusive agreements, consumers are presented with an effective monopoly.

The kinked demand curve model

- The model illustrates the interdependence and uncertainty facing firms and why oligopolistic markets tend to have stable prices and non-price methods of competition.
- If an individual firm produces at Q_1 in Figure 61, selling at price P_1, it perceives its demand curve as being relatively elastic if it raises its price and inelastic if it cuts its price.

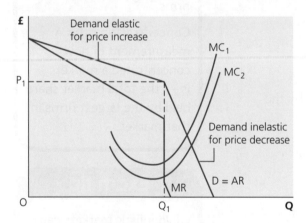

Figure 61 The kinked demand curve model of oligopoly

- Firms expect not to follow a price rise but to follow a price cut.
- If a firm increases its price and rivals do not follow suit, it loses some, but not all, market share.
- If a firm cuts price, other firms have no option but to follow — leading to a small expansion of market size but no increase in market share for the individual firm.
- Firms in an oligopoly prefer non-price forms of competition.

Key terms

Tacit collusion A collusive relationship between firms without any formal agreement having been made.

Overt collusion A collusive relationship between firms involving an open agreement.

Interdependence How firms in a competitive oligopoly are affected by rival firms' pricing and output decisions.

Exam tip

The kinked demand curve model of oligopoly provides a useful illustration of the interdependence and uncertainty facing firms in this form of imperfect competition.

Monopoly

- Pure monopoly exists when there is a single supplier of a good or service, i.e. 100% market share.
- A firm needn't have a pure monopoly to exert monopoly power; there are many industries dominated by a small number of firms with monopoly power.
- Barriers to entry tend to be high.
- Firms restrict output to raise price, which boosts supernormal profits.
- Because of barriers to entry, firms can maintain these profits because new firms can't easily enter the market to compete profits away.

Profit maximisation

- The profit-maximising equilibrium situation for a monopolist is shown in Figure 62.

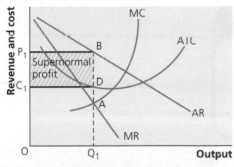

Figure 62 Profit maximisation under monopoly

- As in all market structures, the monopolist maximises profit at the level of output at which $MC = MR$, i.e. at Q_1.
- Firms make supernormal profit equal to the area P_1BDC_1.

Barriers to entry

- A barrier to entry is a feature of a market that makes it difficult for new firms to enter that market and which can therefore lead to **monopoly power**.

> ### Key term
>
> **Monopoly power** The power of a firm in a market to set the ruling market price, known as a price maker.

Type of barrier	Description	Example
Natural barriers	Include naturally occurring climatic, geographical or geological factors that make the product difficult to replicate elsewhere	Wine-growing regions
Economies of scale	When a firm's average costs of production fall as output increases	Large firms can set their prices below those of any potential new entrant firms to the market (becoming the price makers), and still make a supernormal profit
Legal barriers	Factors that give a single firm or individual the right to have a monopoly over a new product, process or other intellectual property, either for ever or over a given time	Patents, copyrights and trademarks
Product differentiation	Existing firms in a market may have spent considerable sums of money over many years on advertising and branding in order to build up a significant consumer loyalty and marketing profile	The large advertising budgets of major soft drinks firms
Sunk costs	Costs that cannot easily be recovered if a firm is unsuccessful in a market and has to exit, i.e. these financial commitments are essentially lost or 'sunk'	Market research costs

Key terms

Product differentiation Using advertising or product design to make a product seem different from those of competitors.

Sunk costs Costs that cannot easily be recovered if a firm is unsuccessful in a market and has to exit.

Advantages and disadvantages

Advantages of a monopoly	Disadvantages of a monopoly
Financial economies of scale	Diseconomies of scale
Technical economies of scale	Productive and allocative inefficiency
Marketing economies of scale	X-inefficiency: the lack of willingness of firms with monopoly power to control their costs of production
Managerial economies of scale	
Innovation	

Productive inefficiency, allocative inefficiency and x-inefficiency under monopoly are shown in Figure 63.

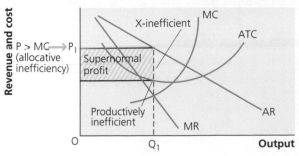

Figure 63 Productive, allocative and x-inefficiency under a monopoly

Price discrimination

- **Price discrimination** is where firms with monopoly power charge different groups of consumers different prices for the same product, allowing a firm to increase its producer surplus at the expense of consumer surplus, as shown in Figure 64.

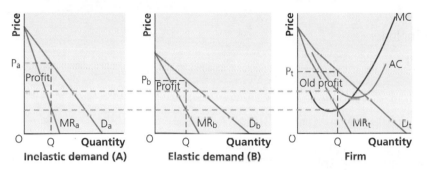

Figure 64 Price discrimination in two separate submarkets, A and B, with the firm as a whole shown in the third set of axes

The conditions necessary for price discrimination are as follows:

- Firms must have a degree of monopoly power.
- Different sub-markets of consumers with different elasticities of demand.
- No 'seepage' between markets — consumers being charged higher prices must not be able to access cheaper prices.

Advantages of price discrimination	Disadvantages of price discrimination
Supernormal profits may be re-invested by the price-discriminating firm, leading to better quality products	Earning or increasing supernormal profit can be seen as inequitable
Extra profits can 'subsidise' those paying a lower price	Increases producer surplus at the expense of consumer surplus
Those on lower incomes can access services, e.g. lower-priced off-peak train fares	May be seen as exploiting those in greatest need who have no choice about using peak-time services

Monopsony

A pure **monopsony** is a firm or organisation that is the sole buyer of resources.

Benefits and costs

Benefits of monopsony	Costs of monopsony
Increased buying power	Suppliers may be forced out of business
Lower buying costs may be passed on to consumers	Reduced consumer choice
Higher profits of monopsony can be used to invest and innovate	Higher profits of monopsony can increase inequality
Can increase buying power in the face of monopoly sellers	May lead to investigation by competition authorities

Key terms

Price discrimination Where firms with monopoly power charge different groups of consumers different prices for the same product.

Monopsony A single, powerful buyer of resources.

Exam tip

Price discrimination isn't always bad for consumers and producers. It may be used to cross-subsidise cheaper prices for less well-off members of society, for example.

Contestability

- **Contestable markets** are those where barriers to entry and exit can be overcome.
- Making markets more contestable could lead to incumbent firms behaving in more economically desirable ways with regard to pricing and static efficiency.

Signs of highly contestable markets include:

- firms entering or leaving the market
- low levels of supernormal profit
- low concentration ratios
- low barriers to entry or exit
- low sunk costs
- firms produce close to where price = marginal cost

Key term

Contestable market A market with freedom of entry and exit.

Do you know?

1 Define the following terms: allocative efficiency, productive efficiency, dynamic efficiency, x-inefficiency.

2 Explain why firms in perfect competition cannot make supernormal profit in the long run.

3 Using at least one diagram, explain the difference between the short run and the long run for a firm in monopolistic competition.

4 Using a diagram, explain how oligopolistic firms may be affected by interdependence.

5 Using a diagram, explain how price discrimination can increase the profits of a monopolist.

3.5 Labour market

You need to know

- demand for labour
- supply of labour
- wage determination

Demand for labour

The demand for factors of production, such as labour, is derived from the demand for the product they are used to create.

- The demand for labour is also known as the theory of **marginal revenue productivity (MRP)**.

Key term

Marginal revenue productivity (MRP) The addition to a firm's revenue from employing an additional unit of a factor of production, usually labour.

- A firm's demand for labour depends on the productivity of additional units of labour, known as **marginal physical product (MPP)**, multiplied by the selling price of the product.
- MRP is the addition to a firm's revenue from employing an additional unit of labour.
- The demand curve for labour, usually referred to as the MRP curve, shows the relationship between the wage rate and the number of workers employed.
- In a perfectly competitive product market, MR is constant and therefore the gradient of the MPP and MRP curves will be the same.

Determinants of labour demand

- Wage rates
- Labour productivity
- The price of substitute factors
- Other labour costs

A change in wage rate will lead to a movement along the demand curve for labour, while a change in the other determinants will lead to a shift of the demand curve for labour.

Determinants of elasticity of demand for labour

- Ease of substitution
- Time
- Elasticity of demand for the good or service
- Proportion of labour cost to total cost of production

The formula for **elasticity of demand for labour** is:

elasticity of demand for labour =

$$\frac{\text{percentage change in quantity of labour demanded}}{\text{percentage change in wage rate}}$$

Supply of labour

- The supply curve for labour shows the relationship between the wage rate and number of workers willing and able to work in a particular occupation.
- It is influenced by monetary factors such as the wage rate and non-monetary factors such as job satisfaction and working conditions.

Determinants of labour supply

- Wage rates
- Size of working population
- Non-monetary factors

A change in wage rate will lead to a movement along the supply curve for labour.

A change in the other determinants will lead to a shift of the supply curve for labour.

Determinants of elasticity of supply of labour

- The elasticity of supply of labour is a measure of the responsiveness of the quantity of labour supplied following a change in the wage rate.
- The formula is:

elasticity of supply of labour =
$$\frac{\text{percentage change in quantity of labour supplied}}{\text{percentage change in wage rate}}$$

- The factors determining the elasticity of supply of labour:
  - ☐ time
  - ☐ the length of training period
  - ☐ vocation

Wage determination

Wage determination in competitive markets

- Features of a perfectly competitive labour market:
  - ☐ each unit of labour is identical in skill and unable to influence the wage rate
  - ☐ workers must accept the going wage rate, determined by supply and demand at market level
  - ☐ individual firms are wage takers
  - ☐ individual firms maximise profit by employing the quantity of labour at which MRP = MC (the wage rate)
  - ☐ perfect information
  - ☐ freedom of entry to and exit from the industry
- In a perfectly competitive labour market, each individual employer has to accept the ruling market wage, as shown in the right-hand diagram in Figure 65.

> ### Exam tip
> Workers will take into account the monetary and non-monetary features of a job when deciding to supply their labour, a concept referred to as 'net advantage'. Good non-monetary factors may compensate for relatively poor pay, and vice versa.

> ### Key term
> Elasticity of supply of labour A measure of the responsiveness of the quantity of labour supplied following a change in the wage rate.

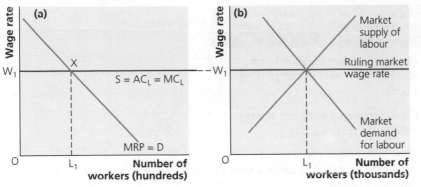

Figure 65 Determination of wages and employment levels in a perfectly competitive labour market. (a) One firm in the market, (b) the whole labour market

Wage determination in non-competitive markets

- This is the situation where either buyers have monopsony power — e.g. NHS employing nurses can force wages down — or suppliers have monopoly power, e.g. trade unions can force wages up.

Minimum and maximum wages

- A minimum wage legally obliges employers to pay workers at least a certain hourly rate.
- Depending upon the elasticities of demand and supply for labour, the introduction or raising of the national minimum wage (NMW) may have significant impacts upon employment levels.
- A maximum wage has been suggested in order to limit the incomes of the highest earners.
- The effects of introducing a minimum wage in a competitive labour market are shown in Figure 66, whereas the effects of a maximum wage are shown in Figure 67.

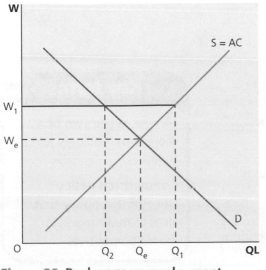

Figure 66 Real wage unemployment

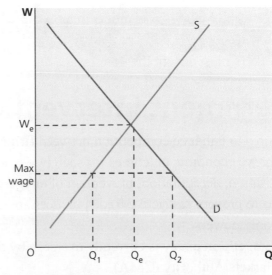

Figure 67 Effects of imposition of a maximum wage

Advantages of minimum and maximum wages	Disadvantages of minimum and maximum wages
Minimum wages can help reduce poverty Maximum wages can prevent the richest in society from getting richer	Minimum wages may lead to a surplus of workers in competitive markets Minimum wages may not always reflect the cost of living Maximum wages may reduce incentives and lead to some workers moving overseas

Do you know?

1 Explain how marginal revenue productivity determines the demand for labour.

2 State three reasons why the demand curve for labour might shift to the right.

3 State three reasons why the supply curve for labour might shift to the left.

4 Explain how wages and employment are determined in a perfectly competitive labour market.

5 Using a diagram, explain the impact of increasing the national minimum wage.

3.6 Government intervention

You need to know
- types of government intervention
- the impact of government intervention

Government intervention

- Measures to enhance competition between firms in order to improve economic outcomes for society, e.g. legislation, privatisation, deregulation, prevention of mergers and various actions to prevent restrictive trade practices and abuse of monopoly power.
- UK competition policy is currently overseen by the Competition and Markets Authority (CMA).

Key terms

Merger When two or more firms willingly join together.

Competition policy Government policy that aims to make markets more competitive.

Principles of UK competition policy

- Competition policy in the UK is focused on four areas:
  - ☐ monopolies
  - ☐ mergers
  - ☐ restrictive trading practices
  - ☐ promoting competition

Intervention to control mergers

- Mergers are when two or more firms willingly join together.
- Competition policy considers whether mergers and takeovers might create a new monopoly.
- Mergers and takeovers may be prohibited if they are predicted to substantially reduce competition.

Intervention to control monopolies

- The CMA uses a structure, conduct and performance approach to judging the relative merits of each investigation it makes.
- Possible approaches to tackling monopolies include:
  - ☐ compulsory break-up
  - ☐ windfall taxes on 'excess' or supernormal profits
  - ☐ price controls such as maximum prices
  - ☐ public ownership (nationalisation)
  - ☐ privatisation
  - ☐ deregulation
  - ☐ enforcing quality standards
  - ☐ setting performance targets

Intervention to promote competition and contestability

Examples of private-sector involvement in public organisations include:

- private finance initiative (PFI)
- contracting out

Deregulation

- **Deregulation** is the removal of rules and regulations in order to increase the efficiency of markets.
- May reduce firms' costs of production, meaning consumers benefit from lower prices.
- The promotion of competition may lead to a more contestable market.
- May avoid the problem of **regulatory capture**.

Competitive tendering for government contracts

- This is when government acquires goods or services by inviting suppliers to bid for a contract.
- In general, the bid with the lowest price wins, leading to better 'value for money' for taxpayers.

Privatisation

The advantages and disadvantages of **privatisation** are summarised below.

Advantages of privatisation	Disadvantages of privatisation
Raising extra revenue for the government	Exploitation of monopoly power
Promoting competition	Short-termism: a focus on cost-cutting to maximise short-term profits rather than on longer-term investment projects
Promoting efficiency	
Encouraging greater share ownership by the general public may lead to greater pressure on firms to act in the public interest	Private firms may ignore the externalities of their activities

Intervention to protect suppliers and employees

Restrictions

- **Regulation** refers to rules and laws that restrict market freedom.
- External regulation involves agencies such as the CMA imposing rules and restrictions.
- Self-regulation involves organisations in particular industries voluntarily regulating themselves, e.g. membership of a professional governing body such as the Institute of Chartered Accountants in England and Wales, or the Law Society.
- While regulation may impose additional costs on businesses, it is felt to be justified in that it protects consumers from abuse of monopoly power and external costs.
- However, regulation may lead to the problem of regulatory capture.

Nationalisation

- **Nationalisation** is when firms, industries or other assets are owned by the government.
- Advantages include:
  - □ nationalised monopolies are more likely to take account of externalities
  - □ state-run monopolies are more likely to produce at an allocatively efficient output
  - □ key industries such as rail, energy, steel and water may be regarded as too important to be run by private organisations

Key terms

Privatisation The sale of government-owned assets to the private sector.

Regulation The imposition of rules and laws that restrict market freedom.

Nationalisation The transfer of assets from the private sector to public ownership.

- Disadvantages of **public ownership** include:
  - □ there can be a lack of dynamic efficiency
  - □ the best managers and leaders are to be found in the private sector, where financial rewards may be significantly higher

The impact of government intervention

- The aims of government intervention are:
  - □ promoting competition between firms
  - □ ensuring firms do not profit to the point of abusing market power
  - □ making markets work more efficiently
  - □ ensuring minimum standards for quality
  - □ preserving choice for consumers
- However, government intervention may fail to improve the allocation of resources if there is regulatory capture or asymmetric information (see Sections 1.3 and 4.4).

> **Key term**
>
> **Public ownership**
> Government ownership of firms, industries or other assets.

Do you know?

1 Explain three policies that could be used to control the actions of monopolies in the UK.
2 Explain the intended impact of government intervention in markets dominated by a small number of firms.
3 Discuss reasons why government intervention to tackle monopolies may fail to achieve an optimal allocation of resources.

End of section 3 questions

1 Define the term 'horizontal integration'.
2 Define the term 'contestable market'.
3 Explain three reasons why groups of workers may earn more than others.
4 Explain why a firm's costs of production may be influenced by diminishing returns in the short run and increasing returns to scale in the long run.
5 Explain why firms in perfectly competitive markets may be productively and allocatively efficient.
6 Explain three possible benefits of privatisation of industries such as the railway or the postal service.
7 Evaluate policy measures the government could use to increase competition in industries such as transport, supermarkets and banking.
8 Evaluate alternative methods that could be used to tackle the market failure associated with energy use.

4 A global perspective

4.1 International economics

You need to know

- what the balance of payments is and its components
- what causes an imbalance on the current account of the balance of payments and how this can be reduced
- how exchange rates are determined and the impact of changes in the exchange rate
- how international competitiveness is measured and its significance

Globalisation

Characteristics of globalisation

- Greater foreign trade
- Higher levels of overseas migration
- Increasing capital flows between countries
- Emergence of global brands
- Greater use of outsourcing/offshoring

Factors contributing to globalisation

- Improvements in transport in speed and cost reduction, e.g. containerisation
- Increased free trade
- Closer political ties
- Abolition of capital controls

Impacts of globalisation and global companies

Globalisation has significant impact on everything from individual countries to the environment, as shown in the following table.

Individual countries	Governments	Producers	Consumers	Workers	The environment
Can specialise in their comparative advantage Higher output possible through specialisations Increased living standards	Tax revenues may increase (though tax avoidance may occur through transfer pricing) Attract 'hard currency' that can be used to settle international transactions	Firms have access to wider markets — more sales Reduce cost of production by outsourcing to low-cost countries Access to modern technologies and management techniques Exploit economies of scale Spread risk by operating in many countries	Wider range of products to choose from Lower prices from global marketplace	Increase employment opportunities due to global labour market Downward pressure on wages due to competition from low-cost producers	Poorer countries may see damage to the environment as resources are exploited Resource depletion may occur

Specialisation and trade

Absolute advantage

This is most easily illustrated by means of an example. Assuming a two country/two product model:

- Each country initially produces both products, with factors of production divided equally between production of food and clothing.

	Food (output in units)	Clothing (output in units)
Country A	300	150
Country B	150	300
World total	450	450

- Country A has absolute advantage in food and country B in clothing — they can produce more than the other country.
- However, if each country were to specialise in its absolute advantage:

	Food (output in units)	Clothing (output in units)
Country A	600	0
Country B	0	600
World total	600	600

- Specialisation increases world output.
- Country A and country B can now trade, making each country better off than before.

Synoptic link

This example can be shown in the form of production possibility frontiers, like those in Section 1.1. However, these assume a constant opportunity cost of production in each country.

■ Specialisation and trade allows each country to consume beyond its own internal PPF. For example, on the diagram, each country could consume 300 units of each (assuming trade takes place on a unit-for-unit swap).

Comparative advantage

In this instance, one country may be better at producing both products.

	Food (output in units)	Clothing (output in units)
Country A	400	800
Country B	200	50
World total	600	850

■ Country A has absolute advantage in both food and clothing.
■ Specialisation can still be beneficial if each country specialises in its comparative advantage.
■ Comparative advantage is measured by the opportunity cost of producing a product in terms of what instead could have been produced in the same country.
  □ In country A: opportunity cost of one unit of clothing is half a unit of food.
  □ In country B: opportunity cost of one unit of clothing is four units of food.
  □ Therefore, country A has comparative advantage in clothing.
  □ In country A: opportunity cost of one unit of food is two units of clothing.
  □ In country B: opportunity cost of one unit of food is a quarter of a unit of clothing.
  □ Therefore, country B has comparative advantage in food.

If each country specialises in its comparative advantage, world output is as follows:

	Food (output in units)	Clothing (output in units)
Country A*	200	1200
Country B	400	0
World total	600	1200

* In this example, country A has partially specialised by putting a quarter of resources into food production and three quarters of resources into clothing production.

■ World output is higher than before specialisation.
■ Trade is mutually beneficial (at an appropriate exchange rate) — each country can consume more, despite one country being less efficient at producing both products.

Assumptions and limitations

- Factor immobility between countries
- Perfect factor mobility within each country
- No economies or diseconomies of scale
- Transport costs — small enough not to matter
- No artificial trade barriers

Advantages and disadvantages of specialisation and trade

Advantages	Disadvantages
Higher incomes/living standards	Increased local unemployment
Lower prices	Infant industries struggling
Increased choice	Over-reliance on primary products
Less dominance by national monopolies	Risk of dumping
Economies of scale for producers	Global monopolies may emerge

Factors influencing pattern of trade

- Comparative advantage — countries specialise in their comparative advantage.
- Impact of emerging economies — a source of cheap imports, but increasingly a destination for exports.
- Growth of trading blocs and bilateral trading agreements, e.g. EU, NAFTA and ASEAN.
- Changes in relative exchange rates.

Terms of trade

$$\text{terms of trade} = \frac{\text{index of export prices}}{\text{index of import prices}}$$

Factors influencing the **terms of trade** include:

- relative productivity in the country compared with its trading partners
- relative inflation in the country relative to its trading partners
- trade protection
- exchange rates

Key term

Terms of trade The ratio of export prices to import prices.

Impact of changes in a country's terms of trade

If terms of trade improve (increase), the following may occur:

- current account balance moves into deficit — as exports become less price competitive
- standards of living improve — as same quantity of exports can finance a larger quantity of imports

Trading blocs and the World Trade Organization (WTO)

Types of trading blocs

Free trade areas — no trade barriers between members but members can form own agreements with nonmembers	**Customs unions** — no trade barriers between members and a common external tariff applied on imports from non-members
Common markets — the same as a customs union with other forms of integration, such as the free movement of labour and capital between members, e.g. the EU	**Monetary unions** — customs unions and common market sharing a common currency and monetary policy (e.g. the Eurozone)

Costs and benefits of regional trade agreements

Costs of regional trade agreements	Benefits of regional trade agreements
Trade diversion	Trade creation
Inability to make trade deals with non-members	Increase in FDI
	Increase in intra-regional trade
Cost of adhering to common rules and product standards	

Key terms

Trading bloc A group of countries (two or more) that agree to remove restrictions on international trade.

Bilateral trade agreements Decisions to reduce trade barriers between two countries.

Regional trade agreements Where countries in close proximity agree to remove trade barriers.

Trade diversion Trade barriers lead to trade occurring with less efficient producers.

Trade creation Trade is increased due to membership of a regional trade agreement.

Role of the WTO in trade liberalisation

- More than 100 countries are WTO members.
- The WTO promotes trade liberalisation across membership.
- Trade negations are conducted in 'rounds'.
- The WTO has been successful in gradually reducing trade barriers.

Conflicts between regional trade agreements and the WTO

- A recent trend has been the growth of regional trade blocs, such as the EU, NAFTA and ASEAN.
- Growth of regional trade agreements conflicts with the general aims of the WTO in promoting free trade across membership.
- A likely solution is for the WTO to forge agreements between trading blocs, e.g. NAFTA with the EU.

Restrictions on free trade

Arguments for protectionist policies	Arguments against protectionist policies
Protection of jobs	Based on comparative advantage, free trade maximises global output
Infant industry — protecting small domestic industries from larger, efficient competition	Protecting infant/sunset industries encourages inefficiency
Anti-dumping — large overseas businesses selling output below cost to drive domestic businesses out	Higher prices (and possible job losses elsewhere due to reduced spending power)
Sunset industries — protecting industries in long-term decline	Protectionist policies usually encourage retaliatory measures
Strategic reasons — protecting strategically important industries, e.g. agriculture	

Types of restrictions on trade

- Tariffs — a tax on imports.
  - ☐ Tariffs increase import prices, encouraging a switch to domestic alternatives, as shown in Figure 68. As the world price rises from P_W to P_T, the quantity of imports falls from Q_1Q_2 to Q_3Q_4.

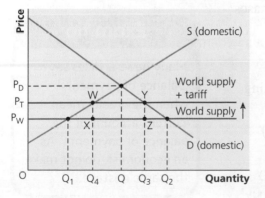

Figure 68 The effects of a tariff on imports

> ### Synoptic link
>
> The tariff diagram uses microeconomic demand and supply diagrams.

- Quotas — a limit on the quantity of imports.
- Export subsidies — governments subsidising export-producing industries.
- Red tape/artificial barriers — lengthy administrative procedures or complex legal standards for imports.

Impact of protectionist policies

On consumers	On producers	On governments	On living standards	On equality
Higher prices, due to tariffs and quotas	Less competition from low-cost producers	Tax revenue received from tariffs	Higher prices and less efficient resource allocation means incomes may fall	May lead to greater equality but mainly due to incomes not rising as quickly

Balance of payments

The balance of payments consists of three sections:

- current account
- capital account
- financial account

Details of the current account are covered in Section 2.1.

- The balance on the total of the three sections affects the foreign currency reserves held by the UK government:
  - □ a balance of payments deficit means reserves fall
  - □ a balance of payments surplus means reserves rise
- A government can alternatively cover a balance of payments deficit by borrowing.
- If foreign reserves are insufficient to finance a current account deficit, surplus must be generated on the financial or capital account.

The capital account contains some capital transfers and purchases/sales of non-financial assets.

There are three components in the financial account:

- foreign direct investment (FDI) — opening up/buying existing business located outside the country of ownership
- portfolio investment — trade in financial assets (e.g. shares) outside the country of ownership
- short-term movements of capital — into and out of a country, often moved for speculative motives and known as 'hot money'

Exam tip

Many news articles say 'balance of payments' when they really mean 'current account of the balance of payments'. As an economist, do not make the same mistake.

Balance on the current account

- The current account balance is measured by difference between inflows and outflows of money into and out of a country due to:
  - ☐ exports and imports
  - ☐ investment income from factors of production located outside their country of ownership
  - ☐ transfers of money between countries
- Current account deficit: outflows > inflows
- Current account surplus: inflows > outflows
- The UK current account is normally in deficit (surplus on services < deficit on goods)

Exam tip

Achieving balance on the current account will not always be high priority and often conflicts with achieving other, more important, objectives.

Causes of current account deficits and surpluses

Cause of current account deficit	Cause of current account surplus
High/rising exchange rate	Low/falling exchange rate
High domestic/low foreign economic growth	High foreign/low domestic economic growth
Low relative productivity	High relative productivity
High relative inflation	Low relative inflation

Key terms

Expenditure-reducing policies Reducing current account deficits through reductions in AD.

Expenditure-switching policies Reducing current account deficits through encouraging a switch away from imports to domestic output.

Measures to reduce a current account deficit

- Achieving the balance on the current account is an economic objective.
- Deficits on the current account can be corrected (eliminated or reduced) by:
  - ☐ **expenditure-reducing policies**
  - ☐ **expenditure-switching policies**

Exam tip

Although achieving balance on the current account is a macroeconomic objective, this is rarely seen as a priority for UK governments.

Expenditure-reducing policy 1: deflation

How it works	Issues with this policy
Reducing UK consumption leads to fewer imports Reductions in UK consumption are achieved by: ■ higher interest rates ■ higher taxes ■ lower government spending	Unpopular with the population Conflicts with objectives for growth and unemployment Higher interest rates may cause a rise in exchange rate which reduces exports

Expenditure-switching policy 1: devaluation

How it works	Issues with this policy
If currency falls (either by devaluation or by depreciation), export prices appear cheaper overseas — so exports should rise If currency falls, import prices rise — so imports should fall	**Marshall–Lerner condition** Devaluation *only* improves the current account balance if the Marshall–Lerner condition is satisfied Marshall–Lerner condition = PED (of exports) + PED (of imports) > 1 If the condition is not satisfied, devaluation will not improve the current account balance at all
This gives us the J curve (shown in Figure 69), where devaluation worsens deficit initially before it improves over time Figure 69 **The J curve**	**The J curve** Devaluation will not immediately improve the balance In the short run, demand for exports and imports is more price inelastic and demand doesn't change much However, imports now cost more, so the value of imports rises Therefore, the current account balance worsens in the short run before improving In the medium term, demand for exports and imports becomes more price elastic — meaning demand for exports rises and demand for imports falls The current account balance eventually improves

Expenditure-switching policy 2: protectionist policies

How it works	Issues with this policy
Trade barriers that prevent free trade lead to lower levels of imports to improve the current account balance Methods used are covered earlier in this section	Protection usually leads to other countries retaliating — reducing UK exports Trade barriers are not allowed in some customs unions, e.g. the EU

> **Synoptic link**
>
> For a devaluation to improve the current account balance, the price elasticity matters — and how this changes over time.

Expenditure-switching policy 3: supply-side policies

How it works	Issues with this policy
Reforming the economy should lead to improvements in exports Improvements to productivity, infrastructure and education should boost exports' competitiveness	It takes many years to have a full effect Difficult to measure

Significance of global trade imbalances

- If governments attempt to eliminate a current account deficit, it will have knock-on effects across the world.
- A fall in spending on imports means a fall in exports from another country.
- Protectionist policies adopted by large economies can significantly affect the growth rate in smaller economies, if they sell fewer exports to the larger economy.

Reasons for wanting to avoid current account deficits

- A large current account deficit can indicate export sector weakness.
- Interest rates may need to rise to generate a surplus on the other parts of the balance of payments.
- Persistent deficits may lead to diminished foreign currency reserves (unless surplus exists on financial or capital accounts).
- If the government has insufficient foreign currency reserves, it may need to:
  - ☐ borrow money
  - ☐ deflate the economy — i.e. reduce AD
- Deficits often lead to falling currency values, which can boost cost-push inflation.

Reasons why current account deficits may not matter

- This objective is usually seen as lower priority than achieving growth, employment and low inflation.
- Current account deficits may be due to high economic growth, which is more desirable.
- A surplus on the financial account — e.g. from FDI — may 'cover' the current account deficit.
- Deficits that are large when measured in £s may be small when measured as a percentage of GDP.

Reasons for wanting to avoid account surpluses

- Current account surplus may be due to low economic growth.
- It may be inflationary if exports rise quickly.
- Foreign countries may introduce protectionist policies.
- It may lead to rising currency.

> ### Exam tip
>
> The size of the current account is normally judged as a percentage of the economy's GDP.

Exchange rates

The government will adopt one of the following three exchange rate systems:

- floating exchange rates: where the government doesn't attempt to influence the value of the exchange rate
- fixed exchange rate: where the government stabilises the exchange rate at a fixed value
- managed exchange rate: where the currency floats but the government will intervene and influence the exchange rate's value on occasion

> **Key term**
>
> **Exchange rate** The price of one currency in terms of another currency.

Revaluation/devaluation and appreciation/depreciation

- A rising currency is said to be strengthening.
- A falling currency is said to be weakening.

When the exchange rate is fixed	When the exchange rate is floating
A rise in the currency's value is known as a revaluation	A rise in the currency's value is known as an appreciation
A fall in the currency's value is known as a devaluation	A fall in the currency's value is known as a depreciation

Factors influencing floating exchange rates

- The exchange rate of floating currencies is determined by demand and supply of the currency, as shown in Figure 70.

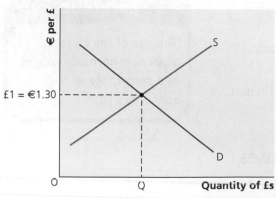

Figure 70 The exchange rate is determined by the demand for and supply of a currency

- A rise in demand for a currency leads to rising exchange rate (and vice versa), as shown by the shift from D_1 to D_2 in Figure 71.
- A rise in supply of a currency leads to falling exchange rate (and vice versa), as shown by the shift from S_1 to S_2 in Figure 72.

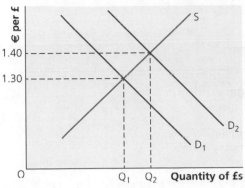

Figure 71 A rise in the demand for the pound will lead to a rise in the exchange rate

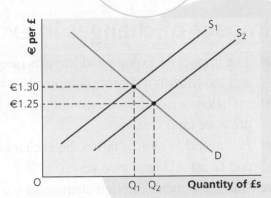

Figure 72 An increase in imports will increase the supply of the pound and lead to a fall in the exchange rate

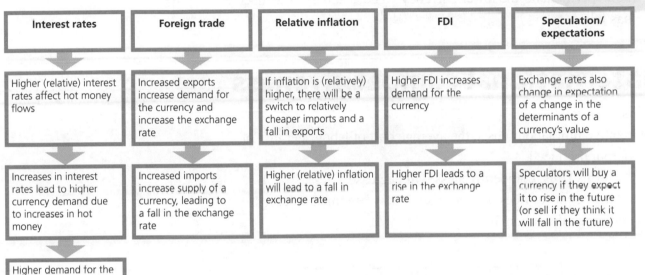

Interest rates	Foreign trade	Relative inflation	FDI	Speculation/ expectations
Higher (relative) interest rates affect hot money flows	Increased exports increase demand for the currency and increase the exchange rate	If inflation is (relatively) higher, there will be a switch to relatively cheaper imports and a fall in exports	Higher FDI increases demand for the currency	Exchange rates also change in expectation of a change in the determinants of a currency's value
Increases in interest rates lead to higher currency demand due to increases in hot money	Increased imports increase supply of a currency, leading to a fall in the exchange rate	Higher (relative) inflation will lead to a fall in exchange rate	Higher FDI leads to a rise in the exchange rate	Speculators will buy a currency if they expect it to rise in the future (or sell if they think it will fall in the future)
Higher demand for the currency leads to an exchange rate increase				

Figure 73 Determinants of the exchange rate

Government intervention in currency markets

This can take place through:

- open-market operations, which involves buying and selling a currency using foreign currency reserves held by the government
- interest rate change — to influence the demand for a currency through flows of 'hot money'

Competitive devaluation/depreciation

- A government might deliberately cause a devaluation or depreciation of its own currency.
- This would boost the competitiveness of its export sector.
- If other countries copy the policy, the gains are cancelled out.
- The end result often is where governments resort to protectionist policies.

Impact of changes in exchange rates

- The impact on exports and imports (see page 104 on the J curve and the Marshall–Lerner condition).
- Inflation: a rising exchange rate means less cost-push inflationary pressure (and vice versa).
- Economic growth: a fall in the exchange rate should boost exports and boost AD (and vice versa).
- Unemployment: through changes in the size of export orientated industries.
- FDI: a lower exchange attracts FDI inflows, but this depends on how 'permanent' the lower currency value is and by how much it has fallen.

International competitiveness

This is measured by:
- relative unit labour costs: the average cost of labour per unit of output produced
  - □ if this rises, competitiveness will decrease
- relative export prices: if these rise, it may become harder to compete internationally

Factors influencing international competitiveness

- Productivity of the workforce
- Unit labour costs
- The real exchange rate (the exchange rate adjusted for changes in price levels over time)
- Non-wage labour costs, e.g. taxes on labour
- Labour market regulation — e.g. laws protecting workers, minimum wage rates
- The level of technology and research and development

Benefits of being internationally competitive	Problems of being internationally uncompetitive
Boost to GDP (via exports)	Lower GDP (lower exports)
Lower unemployment	Higher unemployment
Move towards surplus on current account	Move towards deficit on current account
Rising exchange rate (and lower inflation)	Falling exchange rate (and higher inflation)

4.2 Poverty and inequality

You need to know

■ how poverty is measured and the differences in types of poverty

■ the main causes of poverty

■ how inequality is measured, its causes and consequences

Absolute and relative poverty

Distinction between absolute poverty and relative poverty

■ Those in **absolute poverty** are struggling to survive daily — they cannot afford or access the basic needs for survival. Basic needs for survival include food, clothing, shelter and warmth.

■ **Relative poverty** is where people's incomes fall below a minimum level of income in relation to the average for that country.

■ People in relative poverty can be better off than those in earlier years who were not in relative poverty.

■ In the UK, those working full-time on the minimum wage would, without any other benefits, be on the edge of relative poverty (though they will likely qualify for some 'tax credits').

■ Absolute poverty is more useful when considering developing countries.

■ Relative poverty is more useful when considering developed countries.

Key terms

Absolute poverty Where a person's income falls below that needed to fund the basic needs for survival.

Relative poverty Where a person's income falls below a certain level — usually measured in relation to the average income for that country.

Measures of absolute poverty and relative poverty

- The World Bank classifies absolute poverty if an individual's income falls below $1.90 per day.
- Relative poverty applies to those whose income falls below a set percentage of that country's per capita income.
- In the EU, relative poverty is where income falls below 60% of the per capita income of an individual country.
- A person's income can rise over time, but they can still fall into relative poverty if the average income for their country rises faster.

Causes of poverty

- Relatively low wages
- Unemployment
- Regressive taxation
- Health issues
- Level of indebtedness
- Access to public services
- Welfare system

Inequality

Distinction between wealth and income inequality

- **Wealth inequality** covers how there are differences in the value of the stock of assets held by individuals and households.
- **Income inequality** exists in most economies — as the distribution of income is uneven.

Measurements of income inequality

The Lorenz curve

- The Lorenz curve (Figure 74) looks at the population and how income is shared out by percentage of the population, e.g. what percentage of income is earned by the poorest 20% of the population.
- The 45° line indicates perfect equality of income.
- The concave curve represents the Lorenz curve.
- The more concave the curve is, the greater the level of income inequality.

> ### Key terms
>
> **Wealth inequality** The unequal distribution of assets.
>
> **Income inequality** Where incomes are not equally distributed across the economy.

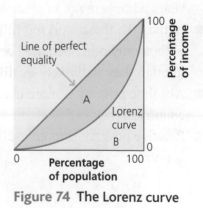

Figure 74 The Lorenz curve

The Gini coefficient

- The Gini coefficient uses information from the Lorenz curve to express inequality as a number.
- Looking at Figure 74, the Gini coefficient is calculated as follows:

$$\frac{\text{area A}}{\text{area A} + \text{B}}$$

- Greater income inequality means area A becomes bigger than area A + B.
- Gini coefficient = 0 means perfect equality of income.
- Gini coefficient = 1 means perfect inequality of income.
- Gini coefficient can be measured based on gross income and net income (with an adjustment for welfare benefits).
- Gini coefficient for household income (income less taxes plus benefits) is smaller than for income before deductions and additions.

Causes of income and wealth inequality

Within countries	Between countries
Differences in skills and education	Natural resources
Generosity of the welfare system	Political stability
Inheritance laws	How open the economy is to foreign trade
How progressive taxation system is	
Wage rates (and the strength of trade unions)	Interference from outside countries
	Macroeconomic policies
Access to the property market	Investment in education and training

Impact of economic change and development on inequality

- Developing economies may initially have reasonably low income inequality.
- During development, income inequality increases.
- Whether continued growth leads to reductions in inequality depends on the views of the population in the economy.
- In recessions, income inequality may increase again (as unemployment significantly increases inequality).

Significance of capitalism for inequality

- Capitalist economies are generally more unequal than non-capitalist economies.
- Owners of the production resources generally see their incomes rising faster than those who do not own significant amounts of resources.
- Returns on wealth are often greater than returns on incomes, meaning wealth inequality increases.
- Wealth inequality can lead to further income inequality, as wealth generates higher incomes.

Do you know?

1 Explain the link between income and wealth.

2 Explain how education can reduce the chances of people ending in poverty.

3 Explain how someone's income can increase but they move into poverty.

4.3 Emerging and developing economies

You need to know

- how development is measured and the uses and limitations of measures used
- what factors lead to growth and development
- what strategies can be used to achieve development

Measures of development

Human Development Index

- The Human Development Index (HDI) is a composite index used by the United Nations. It is based on combined values for:
  - □ real GDP per capita (PPP)
  - □ health — based on life expectancy
  - □ education — based on mean and expected years of schooling

Synoptic link

Disadvantages of HDI include the limitations of using GDP per capital to assess living standards

Advantages and disadvantages of using the HDI

Advantages	Disadvantages
It is a wider measurement than GDP per capita	It is still a narrow measure — only three components
All components are good indicators of development	Does not account for inequality of income
	Quality of education is not included
	Does not include issues relating to human rights, freedom etc.

Other indicators of development

- Human Poverty Index
- Gender-related Development Index (GDI)
- Gender Empowerment Measure (GEM)
- Social indicators, e.g. access to doctors, access to clean water

Factors influencing growth and development

Impact of economic factors in different countries

Primary product dependency

- Primary products are usually more income inelastic in demand.
- Over time, the demand for them will not rise as quickly as income rises.
- Revenues from exports will not rise quickly.

Volatility of commodity prices

- Demand for, and supply of, commodities is price inelastic, making small changes in either result in large price changes.
- Prices of commodities are erratic and may be subject to speculative changes.
- The long-term trend for agricultural prices is downwards (not accepted by all).
- Revenues from agricultural exports will fall over time.
- The terms of trade will deteriorate over time.

Savings gap: Harrod–Domar model

Figure 75 The Harrod–Domar model

Synoptic link

Knowledge of both price elasticity and income elasticity is important for this section.

Foreign currency gap

- Dependency on primary product exports leads to lower export earnings, leading to foreign currency shortages.
- Debt levels in developing countries often require interest to be paid in foreign currency.

Capital flight

- Owners of assets and investments in developing economies may withdraw their money.

Demographic factors

- If population growth exceeds the growth of GDP, GDP per capita must decline.
- If population is ageing, those in work will need to support larger elderly populations.
- Future workforces may have to pay higher taxes, retire later or pension payments must fall if this trend continues.

Debt

- Debt can increase due to dependency on dwindling earnings from primary exports.
- Debt can increase due to low foreign currency earnings making it harder to repay the debt.
- Debts may have increased on inappropriate projects, e.g. military investments rather than additions to the productive capacity of an economy.

Access to credit and banking

- Development will need a thriving business sector in an economy.
- A financial system will need to support saving and borrowing if funds are to be channelled to those wanting to set up or expand a business.

Infrastructure

- Physical, financial and legal systems are needed to support economic activity.
- Structures to support efficient transport, the generation and supply of power and smooth communications make it easier for development to occur.

Education/skills

- Literacy and numeracy are key to enhancing worker productivity.
- Improvements in education can increase workforce productivity and reduce labour immobility.

Absence of property rights

- Property rights are essential for business activity.
- Enforcement of laws and contracts are necessary for business activity.
- Without clear property rights, business activity will be limited.

Impact of non-economic factors in different countries

- Civil unrest — internal conflict, wars
- Political instability — unstable political regimes
- Corruption — in business and political office
- Climate issues
- Colonial interference — from a more powerful economy
- Cultural factors — empowerment of women

Strategies influencing growth and development

Market-orientated strategies and interventionist strategies are summarised in the following table.

Market-orientated strategies	Interventionist strategies
Trade liberalisation — the removal of trade barriers and other obstacles to free trade	Development of human capital — through education and training
Promotion of FDI — policies to attract more FDI, e.g. the promotion of macroeconomic stability and the relaxation of rules of foreign ownership of business	Protectionism — of infant industries or strategic industries
	Managed exchange rates — to maintain a competitive value of the currency
Removal of government subsidies — which could create inefficiency in businesses	Infrastructure development — to increase and enhance the economy's productive capacity
Floating exchange rates — remove the need for holding large quantities of currency reserves and allow for currency depreciation to help competitiveness	Promoting joint ventures with global companies — to increase FDI and learn from these companies
Microfinance — schemes to lend relatively small sums of money for business start-ups, often aimed at women	Buffer stock schemes — to stabilise prices

Other strategies

- Industrialisation — the Lewis model
  - ☐ According to the Lewis model, developing economies have two sectors:
    - agricultural sector — rural based, low productivity, large population
    - industrial sector — urban based, high productivity, small population
  - ☐ Development can only occur if workers transfer from the agricultural to the industrial sector
  - ☐ Investment in the industrial sector will drive up wages and will attract workers to that sector
- Development of tourism — which brings jobs created by MNCs, increased tax revenue, foreign currency earnings and multiplier effects on local businesses
- Development of primary industries — which may attract FDI
- Fairtrade schemes — guaranteeing a fair price for local producers
- Aid — in monetary or non-monetary form
- Debt relief — either improvements in terms of debt conditions or full or part-cancellation of debt

Role of international institutions and non-government organisations

World Bank

- Originally designed to provide long-term loans for reconstruction and development.
- Now focuses on promoting poverty reduction across the world.
- Encourages countries to adopt market-based macroeconomic policies.
- Criticised that its advice often increases inequality.

International Monetary Fund (IMF)

- Designed to provide loans and financial assistance for countries in need.
- Members pay a fee to join.
- Provides financial advice for countries experiencing economic problems.

NGOs

- Non-government organisations (NGOs) focus on community-based programmes designed to further development in countries.

4.4 The financial sector

Role of financial markets

- Financial markets move money from people with a surplus (savers) to those with a shortage (borrowers).
- Financial markets enable:
  - individuals and firms to borrow
  - governments to finance budget deficits
  - international trade

The roles of the various financial markets

Facilitate saving

- Households and businesses save money in financial institutions.
- Most save with commercial banks or building societies.
- Savers receive interest.

Lending to businesses and individuals

- Savings by households allows funds to be lent to businesses, which borrow for start-up and expansion.

Facilitate the exchange of goods and services

- Without banks, transactions between consumers and businesses would be more difficult — especially if high value.

- Transfers of money can be made involving households, businesses, employers and governments across the world easily and quickly.
- Transactions are frequently completed without the use of notes and coins.
- Banks can transfer money between two parties in many ways:
  - ☐ Debit card, cheque, contactless payment, automated transfer, direct debit, standing order.

Provide forward markets in currencies and commodities

- If businesses are worried about the value of a currency changing in the future, the forward market allows them to buy currency in the future but at an agreed rate today.

Provide a market for equities

- Financial markets allow equities (shares in companies) to be issued by businesses raising finance.
- Equities already issued are also traded by investors.

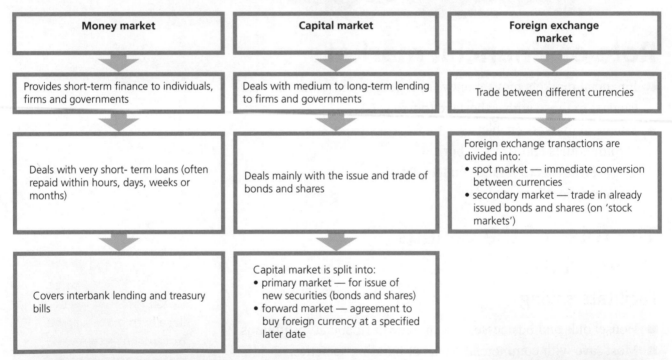

Figure 76 The main financial markets

Market failure in the financial sector

Asymmetric information

- Asymmetric information is where investors know less about the risks of an investment than those selling the financial assets.

Key term

Asymmetric information
Where one party in a transaction has more information about the transaction, giving them an unfair advantage in the terms of the transaction.

- It also refers to when people know 'inside information' about future business performance to help make better decisions about buying and selling equities (insider trading is illegal).

Externalities

- Housing bubbles (one of the most common forms of speculative bubble) developed in the run-up to the 2008 global financial crisis.
- The housing bubble helped to increase inequality — a form of market failure where people cannot access affordable housing due to accelerating prices.

> **Key term**
>
> **Speculative bubble** A speculative (or market) bubble occurs when asset prices (typically houses, commodities and share prices) rise rapidly beyond what normal demand and supply conditions would predict.

Moral hazard

Banks will face cash shortages if those it lends to fail to repay (by defaulting) → If customers think the bank is short of cash, a 'run' on the bank may occur → Runs on banks become self-fulfilling the fear of banks running out of cash encourages more customers to withdraw their cash → The central bank can provide liquidity if the failure of a bank is against the public interest → Knowing a bank can be 'bailed out' creates a moral hazard and banks take too many risks knowing they will not be allowed to fail

Speculation and market bubbles

Speculative bubbles can emerge if credit is easily obtainable for buying assets → Central banks often cannot prevent the bubble developing as it is not part of their remit → Once a bubble bursts, prices of the asstes may collapse and this can leave banks unable to collect the amounts owing to them → Bubbles often develop due to the herding instinct among investors — i.e. investors follow each other's behaviour

Market rigging

- Traders may attempt to fix interest rates in a market so as to make profit on the foreknowledge of where the rate may end up.
- This is highly illegal — some traders have been convicted of market rigging.

> **Key term**
>
> **Market rigging** Where market rates are fixed illegally to make a profit for those investors who can influence and change market rates.

> **Synoptic link**
>
> Market failure was originally covered in Section 1 — it also applies here.

Role of central banks

Implementation of monetary policy

■ The main feature of monetary policy is the setting of interest rates (the Bank rate).

■ Other aspects of monetary policy include:
  □ size of the money supply — see 'quantitative easing' in Section 2.6
  □ availability of credit
  □ exchange rate

■ The Bank of England sets interest rates independently of UK government influence.

■ Objectives of monetary policy:
  □ inflation target (measured by changes in CPI) of 2% per year (±1%)
  □ inflation target is achieved through changes in the Bank rate decided by the Monetary Policy Committee (MPC)
  □ other objectives include full employment and steady economic growth

Banker to the government

■ The Bank of England acts as the banker to the government.

■ Since gaining independence in interest rate setting, some of the roles are now performed by the Debt Management Office.

Banker to the banks: lender of last resort

■ The Bank of England provides money for financial institutions if they cannot gain money anywhere else.

■ The role of the 'lender of last resort' does not mean that it will always lend money; this is the case only if failure of the financial institution is against the public interest.

Role in regulation of the banking industry

■ Until the 2008 financial crisis, regulation of the financial system was limited.

■ Limited regulation was blamed for magnifying the financial crisis.

■ The Financial Services Act 2012 introduced regulatory institutions designed to improve financial stability, as shown in the following table.

Prudential Regulation Authority (PRA)	Financial Policy Committee (FPC)	Financial Conduct Authority (FCA)
Responsible for the supervision of banks and other financial institutions	Monitors, identifies and acts to remove systematic risk from the financial system	Protects consumers by ensuring healthy competition between banks
Takes actions to ensure these are managed properly and can make recommendations of action	Stress tests are conducted to see how 'healthy' the banking sector is	Can intervene and set standards of behaviour if needed
Allows banks to fail if it doesn't disrupt the whole financial system		Independent of the government
		Concerned with macroprudential regulation whereas the PRA and FPC are concerned with microprudential regulation

Liquidity and capital ratios

- Liquidity ratios require banks to hold a percentage of their deposits in liquid form (i.e. as cash or as balances held at the Bank of England) — this restricts bank lending.
- Increases in the liquidity ratio means banks cannot create as much credit and will lend less.
- Liquidity ratios should ensure banks have sufficient liquidity in case of a shortage.
- Capital ratios limit a bank's lending to a percentage of the bank's capital or equity issued. This limits lending by banks compared with their own permanent capital.
- In 2019, the Liquidity Coverage Ratio will be introduced for UK banks — capital must be equal to no less than 7% of their own lending.

Issues with regulation

- Financial crises often affect the whole banking sector (or spread from one bank to others).
- After a crisis, banks often become unwilling to lend.
- Reduced lending has negative effects on the whole macroeconomy.
- Tighter regulation should reduce chances of another crisis.
- Tighter controls restrict people/businesses borrowing.
- Regulation may divert financial activities contributing to GDP to other countries.
- Regulation requires time and money to plan, implement and monitor.
- Penalties are needed to deter excessive risk-taking.
- Unintended consequences are likely.

Synoptic link

Government failure — covered in Section 1.4 — can also occur with excessive regulation.

Do you know?

1 Explain what the difference is between the spot market and the forward foreign exchange market.

2 Distinguish between the primary and secondary capital markets.

3 State three problems of tighter regulation of banks.

4.5 Role of the state in the macroeconomy

You need to know

- the different types of public expenditure and the reasons for them
- the different types of taxes used and the effects of changes in these taxes
- the meaning of the fiscal (budget) balance and the causes of deficits and surpluses, as well as the effect on the economy
- the effects of changes in policy, as well as the limitations of the policies used

Public (government) expenditure

Key terms

Current expenditure Spending on day-to-day costs in providing public services, e.g. NHS salaries.

Capital expenditure Spending on long-term projects, e.g. infrastructure.

Transfer payments Include welfare and benefits.

Reasons for the changing size and composition of public expenditure

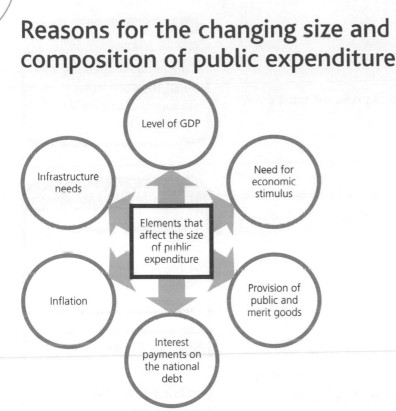

The significance of differing levels of public expenditure as a proportion of GDP

Productivity and growth

■ Large levels of public expenditure can lead to lower economic growth as improvements in productivity are usually lower in the public sector compared with the private sector.

Living standards

■ Public expenditure on health, education, welfare and pensions should boost living standards.
■ Public spending on defence and military does not lead to widespread improvements in living standards.

Crowding out

■ A large public sector may lead to crowding out in one of two ways:
  □ Scarce resources used by the public sector — e.g. skilled labour — can no longer be used by private enterprise.
  □ Higher public expenditure may lead to a higher fiscal deficit, leading to higher interest rates and lower GDP as a result.

Level of taxation

- Higher public expenditure will need higher taxation to finance the spending.
- Deficits can increase in the short run, but tax revenue must cover public expenditure in the long run.

Equality

- Larger public expenditure may mean greater equality, as there is likely to be higher spending on welfare and other things that raise the income of low earners.
- The link between public expenditure and equality may not exist if, for example, there is large military expenditure.

Taxation

- Taxation is one of the main instruments of a government's fiscal policy and finances government expenditure. It can consist of either:
  - ☐ direct taxes — taxes on different forms of income
  - ☐ indirect taxes — taxes on expenditure

Progressive, proportional and regressive taxes

Taxes can be progressive, regressive or proportional.

Progressive taxes	Regressive taxes	Proportional taxes
Progressive taxes are paid in bands of income In the UK, 0%, 20%, 40% and 45% tax rates are used as incomes rise	Taxes on expenditure and fixed-sum taxes are often regressive if the expenditure is paid by all income earners in similar amounts VAT may be regressive if necessities are taxed	VAT may be proportional if only luxuries are taxed

Objectives of taxation

- Raise revenue to finance expenditure.
- Change patterns of economic activity — taxes on demerit goods.
- Redistribute income (possibly via progressive taxes).
- Manage the macroeconomy (to change AD).
- Raise money for particular causes — hypothecated taxes.

Cuts in public spending can boost the economy, via supply-side cuts in benefits.

Key terms

Fiscal policy Changes in government spending or taxation to achieve economic change.

Direct taxes Taxes that cannot be avoided and are normally levied on incomes.

Indirect taxes Taxes that can be passed on to others and are normally on expenditure.

Progressive taxes Taxes that increase as a proportion of income as income rises.

Regressive taxes Taxes that increase as a proportion of income as income falls.

Proportional taxs Taxes that are paid as an equal proportion of income at all levels of income.

Main taxes used in the UK

- Income tax — paid on income from employment
- National insurance contributions
- Corporation tax
- Capital gains tax
- Inheritance tax
- Value added tax (VAT)
- Excise duties
- Council tax
- Stamp duty

The economic effects of changes in tax rates

Changes in direct tax rates	Changes in indirect tax rates
Higher taxes on income can create work disincentives	Changes to indirect taxes can be regressive, e.g. VAT increases
Making direct taxes progressive can make the distribution of income more equal	Changes to indirect taxes can change patterns of consumption
Cuts in direct taxes on businesses and workers can be used to boost AD, leading to higher GDP and lower unemployment	Market failures can be corrected by changes in indirect taxes
Cuts in taxes on businesses can attract FDI into the economy	Higher indirect taxes lead to lower AS in the short-term, leading to lower GDP and higher unemployment
Cuts in direct taxes may be inflationary, but only if the economy is already experiencing high economic growth	Higher indirect taxes are likely to lead to higher prices due to businesses passing on the tax increase as higher prices

The Laffer curve

- Cuts in income tax are a supply-side policy.
- Lower income tax rates mean workers keep more of each £ earned.
- This encourages more people to supply their labour and will increase the tax revenue earned as more people work.
- This is shown on the Laffer curve diagram (Figure 77); cuts in income tax rates will increase tax revenue until the tax rates reach T*.

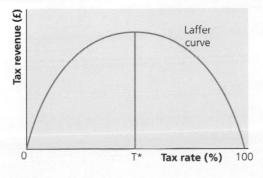

Figure 77 The Laffer curve, showing how lower rates of tax can actually increase tax revenue

Public-sector finances

- The **fiscal balance** measures the difference between government spending and revenue from taxation:
    - ☐ fiscal deficit = government spending > taxation
    - ☐ fiscal surplus = government spending < taxation
- Fiscal balance measures a government's fiscal stance (how 'easy'/'loose' or 'tight'/'restrictive' current policy is).

Automatic stabilisers and discretionary fiscal policy

- **Automatic stabilisers** change the level of AD without the government changing policy.
- If GDP rises, the following occurs:
    - ☐ Government spending on benefits will fall as more people are likely to find jobs.
    - ☐ Tax revenue will rise as more people are working and more people are spending incomes.
- Automatic stabilisers mean that AD is automatically increased or decreased to stabilise the economy:
    - ☐ Automatic stabilisers have more impact if taxes are progressive.
    - ☐ **Discretionary fiscal policy** occurs when there are deliberate attempts to influence the level of AD by changes in tax rates or the level of government spending.

Fiscal deficit and the national debt

- Fiscal deficits are financed by the issue of bonds adding to **national debt**.
- Each fiscal deficit means a higher national debt, measured in money terms.
- Fiscal surpluses allow the partial repayment of national debt.
- Interest on the national debt means more needs to be spent out of tax revenue in 'servicing' the national debt.

Key terms

Fiscal balance The difference between government spending and revenue from taxation.

Automatic stabilisers Changes in fiscal policy that result from changes in GDP rather than deliberate changes by the government.

Discretionary fiscal policy Deliberate changes by the government to levels of public expenditure or tax rates.

National debt The accumulated stock of outstanding bonds issued due for eventual repayment.

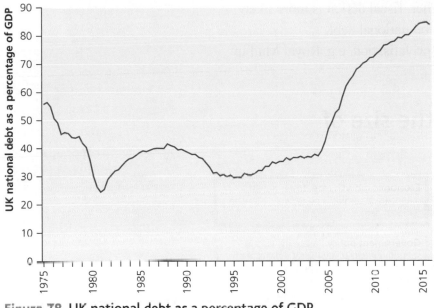

Figure 78 UK national debt as a percentage of GDP

Structural and cyclical deficits

- A fiscal deficit can be caused by:
  - ☐ expansionary fiscal policy
  - ☐ low economic growth leading to low taxation revenue
- Fiscal deficits can be analysed into two components: structural deficits and cyclical deficits.

Structural deficits	Cyclical deficits
Are fiscal deficits remaining when economic growth is average or above?	Are fiscal deficits resulting from lower than average economic growth?
Faster economic growth reduces a fiscal deficit, but the structural component remains	When economic growth is lower than average, taxation revenue falls and government welfare spending increases
Structural deficits are eliminated by reductions in government spending or increases in tax rates	Cyclical deficits are eliminated by faster economic growth

Factors influencing the size of fiscal deficits

- Growth rate of the economy — lower growth leads to fiscal deficits.
  - ☐ Higher growth means less spending on welfare due to low(er) unemployment and higher tax revenues.
  - ☐ Low growth means more spending on welfare and lower tax revenues.
- Government plans for public services (e.g. the expansion of the NHS) mean higher spending will add to a fiscal deficit.
- Expenditure on capital projects (e.g. railways) increase the fiscal deficit.

> **Key terms**
>
> **Structural deficits** Budget deficits that remain even when economic growth is average or higher.
>
> **Cyclical deficits** Budget deficits caused by the effects of lower economic growth.

> **Exam tip**
>
> It is not always easy to judge whether a deficit is cyclical or structural.

- Interest rates on bonds — if higher, fiscal deficit is more likely due to higher interest payments on national debt.
- Sales of publicly owned assets (privatisation, e.g. Royal Mail in 2013).

Factors influencing the size of national debts

Fiscal policy: • Deficits add to the national debt • Surpluses reduce the national debt	Economic growth rate: faster growth means fiscal surplus is more likely, allowing national debt to fall
Credit rating of the country: higher credit rating means lower interest rates on bonds issued	Government policy: 'austerity' cuts in spending mean smaller fiscal deficits, with national debt rising less quickly

The significance of fiscal deficits and surpluses

Economic growth

- Fiscal deficits add to AD and increase economic growth, whereas fiscal surpluses reduce AD and reduce economic growth.
- The rate of economic growth also affects the fiscal balance:
  - Faster growth generates higher tax revenue and reduces a deficit (or adds to a surplus).
  - Lower growth generates lower tax revenue and adds to a deficit (or reduces a surplus).

Unemployment

- Expansionary fiscal policy increases deficit and reduces unemployment.
- Contractionary fiscal policy decreases deficit and increases unemployment.

Inflation

- Expansionary fiscal policy adds to AD and increases demand-pull inflation.
- Contractionary fiscal policy reduces AD and decreases demand-pull inflation.

National debt

- National debt represents accumulated past fiscal deficits.
- Larger national debt means higher interest payments to service this debt (paid on each bond issued).

- If national debt becomes too large, investors buying bonds will demand higher interest rates on each bond issued, increasing government spending.
- National debt (as a percentage of GDP) falls if it grows at a slower rate than the rate of growth in GDP (economic growth).

Macroeconomic policies in a global context

Use of policies

Measures to reduce fiscal deficits and national debts	Measures to reduce poverty and inequality	Changes in interest rates and the supply of money
Increasing public expenditure Increasing taxes Stimulating economic growth (to boost tax revenue)	Making the taxation system more progressive Increasing the level of benefits Increasing the minimum wage Improving the quality of and access to education Reducing unemployment	The effects of changes in interest rates are discussed in Section 2.2 Increased money supply was used as a response to the financial crisis in the form of quantitative easing Interest rate changes are used to keep inflation close to its target level Interest rates can be used to stimulate economic growth if this is a concern (i.e. after the 2008 crisis)

Measures to increase international competitiveness involve policies to reduce a current account deficit. These are discussed in Section 4.1.

Use and impact of macroeconomic policies to respond to external shocks

- External shocks affect real GDP, unemployment and inflation.
- Shocks are either demand-side or supply-side (or both).
- Demand-side shocks affect AD.
  - Examples include the 2008 global financial crisis, a large fall in the exchange rate or the bursting of an asset price bubble.
- Supply-side shocks affect LRAS.
  - Examples include sudden oil price rises, a significant crop failure or large change to prices of an important commodity.

Key term

External shock An unexpected, sudden or large change to aggregate demand or aggregate supply.

Synoptic link

Supply-side shocks caused by large changes in commodity prices are often caused by highly inelastic demand and supply curves.

Measures to control global companies' operations

Regulation of transfer pricing

- Regulation against transfer pricing has proved difficult.
- International agreement would be required if regulation were to occur.
- An alternative approach would be for companies to pay tax on sales in each country.

Limits to government ability to control companies

- Governments often need businesses to come to their country to bring jobs and tax revenue.
- Companies can move between countries if they are unhappy with government policy.
- Many companies are larger in income than entire (albeit, smaller) economies.

Problems facing policymakers when applying policies

- Inaccurate information:
  - □ forecasts are often inaccurate and there are time lags in the data being available, as well as the time lag in terms of the effects of a policy change
- Risks and uncertainties:
  - □ there are multiple possible outcomes for economic variables
  - □ uncertainty will surround most events and outcomes
- Inability to control external shocks:
  - □ shocks by their very nature are unexpected
  - □ the magnitude of a shock makes it difficult to respond to

Do you know?

1 Explain how higher growth can eliminate a fiscal deficit.
2 Explain how the government can stimulate the economy without changing policy.
3 State three methods used to reduce poverty.

End of section 4 questions

Short questions

1 Define the term 'floating exchange rate'.

2 Define the term 'market rigging'.

3 Distinguish between a cyclical and a structural fiscal deficit.

Longer questions

1 Assess the impact of a shift in taxes away from direct to indirect taxes. (9 marks)

2 Discuss the effectiveness of methods taken by a government to reduce types of unemployment that are not cyclical. (15 marks)

3 Assess the impact of a fall in the value of a currency on an economy. (15 marks).

Essay-style question

1 To what extent are current account deficits harmful for an economy? (25 marks)